MO[illegible] ES

[illegible] TETTS

HENRY E. WALTER LTD.

ISBN 0 85479 560 X

First published 1971
Reprinted 1975
Reprinted 1976
Reprinted 1978

Published by
Henry E. Walter Ltd.
Grafton Road, Worthing
and Printed in Great Britain by
Whitstable Litho Ltd., Whitstable, Kent.

Foreword

It gives me the greatest pleasure to commend this book of services. It is one of the fruits of its author's more than forty years of most devoted service to our Lord and to the boys and girls of East London whom he taught, both as assistant and as headmaster. All who bear responsibility in arranging collective worship for young people will find it most helpful.

H. John Scrogie,
Staff Inspector for Religious Education,
Inner London Education Authority.

Contents

Introduction

The services in this book conform to a regular pattern as this helps to produce a serene atmosphere so essential in the morning Act of Worship. A regular order of service prevents children being taken unawares. If variations are made for a special occasion, such as the presentation of Gideon New Testaments, the altered order should be visible for all to see.

This series of services is based on the thematic approach, the theme being based on *stories* from life both past and present, in parable form. Children from homes where there is no belief in God sometimes show their unbelief, in a large gathering such as morning assembly, by remaining silent. A topical or relevant incident from everyday life catches the interest of these children too, for it is both real and personal. The hymn, the scripture reading and the prayer all sustain the theme throughout the Act of Worship.

One of these stories told to a class a week beforehand, would enable them to mime the story whilst it is being told or read, or enable them to re-write it and present it in dramatic form. Alternatively, after such an assembly, R.E. teachers could ask their children to enact the story.

Many of these stories can be used more than once, each time with a different application; e.g., 'Fellow-Workers' besides illustrating 'Choice of Vocation', can be used to illustrate 'Man Keeping a Promise', 'God keeping His Promises' 'Good Example' and 'Life More than Meat'.

The *Bible Reading* should not be omitted. Just as Christ taught divine truths by events from the life of the day, so here the main purpose is to instil in the children's minds, through the modern parable, the teaching behind the *key-verse* from the Bible reading. This should eventually make them realize that they can go to God through the Bible or by prayer for the answer to every problem of their lives. Repetition of the key-verse at the end of the talk will underline the theme. For the maximum effect, reminders by the staff should follow during the day, at appropriate moments. Any visual object which will help to draw the attention of the children and lead their thoughts into the theme, should be used.

Suitable music before the service, or before or during the story-telling, helps to maintain the interest.

The *Hymns* have been chosen for their suitability, and when one is being announced, the line most applicable to the theme from any verse should also be read. All these hymns are well-known and can be found in most hymn-books. Beaumont's Twentieth Century music to some of these is popular with children as this affords a more modern rhythm and melody than the traditional church music, but it should not be used exclusively. Slides of the words projected on to a large screen are more economical than hymn-books and save the time spent in distribution and collection, and are more interesting than hymn-sheets.

Prayer is talking to God. Daily, individual prayers will be encouraged if the leader gives a minute of silence for these before reading the set prayer. Extempore prayer by the leader is better where he has drawn a different moral from the story. Our Lord's Prayer, or another like that of St. Ignatius Loyola, should be added, or used in place of the prayers printed, where it is thought to be more suitable. In time, these prayers will be memorized and become a real help in times of anxiety or distress. Children's written prayers should be included as often as possible, and requests for prayers for personal, family, national or universal needs must be met immediately.

The use of as many as possible of the school staff in leadership is recommended, as this imparts to the children that Christian worship is for the family as well as the individual.

This book should enable assistant teachers who are Christians with a sincere desire to pass on the gospel, but unused to taking assembly, to feel confident of doing so.

All these stories have been used effectively in school

assembly. The words of scripture on which these stories have been based, have set the tone, the standard and the authority for the school.

These services, though presented with the secondary school pupil in mind, are suitable for primary school children also, and for ministers, laymen, or Sunday School teachers seeking material for a children's address where the age-range is wide.

Jesus spent much time in prayer before presenting the Word. So should we.

Index of Bible Readings

Index of Prayers

Index of Services

Acknowledgements

I wish to record my indebtedness to school inspectors, head and assistant teachers, Sunday School teachers, ministers and lay preachers for stories they have told over forty years and to writers and titles forgotten for the germs of illustrations or prayers that I have used.

1. All Power is a Trust

A PARABLE OF TRUST

Scripture Reading: Luke 4:1–14.
Key Verse: 14. Jesus returned in the power of the Spirit.
Hymn: Through all the changing scenes of life.

When I arrived in school this morning the caretaker asked me to accompany him to a classroom. There he showed me the lid of a new desk. Some boy had taken his penknife and carved his initials roughly into the once clean, unspoiled wood. You all know that knives can be put to a good or a bad use and that what this boy had done was not good. This reminded me of a story.

In the year 1800, a boy named Peter Abbott attended Westminster School. As this was near the famous Abbey, Peter and his chums often went there at lunch-time or after school. There was so much to see, the rainbow colours slowly moving across the floor when the sun shone through the stained-glass windows, the many different chapels, especially King Henry VII's with a stall for each knight and his flag hanging above, and of course the famous chair, where for over 600 years the kings and queens of England have been crowned, and under which was the stone believed to be the one that Jacob, Abraham's grandson, used for a pillow.

Peter wanted above all to sit in that chair and imagine himself a king at his coronation, but he was afraid to try it when people and attendants were about. The urge was so strong that one day after school he entered and walked around until closing time. He quite enjoyed dodging around pillars to avoid beng seen. At last all seemed quiet and he felt that it was safe to sit in the chair and this he did. He felt a bit of a thrill for a moment but soon got tired of it and made for the doors to go home. But they were all shut fast. He had been locked in!

He really got quite fed-up with the Abbey by the time that it got dark, and though the Coronation Chair was roomy, and he curled up in it when he got sleepy, it wasn't really comfortable. So he was wide awake by the time the dawn began to light up the Abbey again. But there was still a long time to go before the doors opened again. He looked through his pocket for something to eat or something to play with, and found his penknife. He decided to let the world know that he had spent a night in the Coronation Chair, so he carved these words into the back, '*Peter Abbot slept in this chair, July 5th, 1800*'.

If you go to the Abbey you may see this for yourself, for this is a true story. A lovely, precious chair was spoilt by a silly boy who didn't realize that *all power is a trust*. His knife gave him power, power to spoil, but it should never have been given to him because he couldn't be trusted to use it properly. It gave him the power to cut his quill pen and those of his friends to help them to do better writing, but it also gave him the power to deface and to spoil a valuable chair which was not his property. All power, however small, is a trust.

Jesus had more power than anyone who ever lived. He walked on the sea, stilled a storm, fed 5,000 people on a boy's lunch, turned water into wine, cured the blind and the lame, healed the sick and brought at least three people back from death. His Father God gave Him this power because he knew that Jesus could be trusted not to abuse it. Right at the beginning of His ministry the devil tempted Him three times to use His miraculous powers to serve His own ends. 'Turn these stones into bread, and the thought of food without work will cause all the people to follow you.' 'Throw yourself off the highest pinnacle of the Temple and when you land as gently as a bird on the ground, the people will know that you must be God's Son.' 'Use your power to make the whole world follow you. You have only to say the word. Think how marvellously powerful you will feel then.' But Jesus refused to use His power for the wrong purpose. He replied, 'Get away Satan you mustn't tempt Me.'

What power have you got? Have you, got a knife like Peter Abbott? Can you be trusted not to abuse the power that it gives you? As Jesus knew the secret let us ask Him to help us.

Prayer: Lord Jesus, the desire to use the little power we have to wrong purpose is strong within us. Fill us with Your own Holy Spirit, that these desires may fade and die. *Amen.*

2. *Power from Authority*

A PARABLE OF AUTHORITY

Scripture Reading: Matthew 8:5–10, 13.
Key Verse: 9. I am a man *under* authority.
Hymn: Hail, to the Lord's anointed.

When I was a small boy my father took me one Sunday morning to Woolwich Barracks where I saw the soldiers go on church parade, with a fine band leading the marching and the big-drummer wearing a leopard's skin. It was all grand, especially the way that every soldier in that vast company obeyed the commands of one who was only a sergeant-major. The colonel was present with his fine, feathered hat, but he didn't give the commands, and I wondered why so many men obeyed an under officer.

Many years later, as a sports-master in an Approved School, I was responsible for a physical education display in which every boy in the school had to take part. It was an open day when many important visitors, including the Minister for Home Affairs would be present, and I hoped and prayed that every boy would implicitly obey my every command. I need not have feared. They obeyed well.

Later that evening when the visitors had all gone, I asked one lad who was not usually so obedient, what he thought made everyone obey my commands so perfectly. He said, 'It wasn't so much you sir, but who you stood for, the head-master, the police, the magistrates and the law that were behind you.' That helped me to understand why the soldiers on church parade so long ago obeyed the sergeant-major. Behind him the soldiers saw the officers, the colonel, the king himself, even though he wasn't present.

This should help us to understand why the centurion in this Bible story was obeyed, not that he had much authority, but that he was *under* authority, behind his command was all the authority of the mighty Roman Empire.

Before I became a master I had to be a pupil. Before we become officers we have to be privates. We have to learn to obey before we can give orders and expect to be obeyed. We don't elect as the new captain of our team a player who would never obey the one who had been captain over him.

Jesus had the power and the authority to heal the centurion's servant because he had learnt to obey His Father God. Jesus was always telling His disciples to obey the law, even to pay the taxes the Romans imposed upon them.

The mistake some students make when they revolt against authority is that they can't exercise authority until they have learnt to be subject to it, *under* authority.

Paul writing to the Christians in Thessalonica said (1 Thes. 12), 'Pay proper respect to those whom the Lord has chosen to guide and instruct you.' To the Hebrews the apostle said, 'Obey them that rule over you and submit yourselves.' (Heb. 13:17.) To the Romans (13:1), Paul said, 'All legitimate authority is derived from God's authority and the present authority is appointed under God.' These things were said by a man who once persecuted Christians but later came to say, 'Lord, what wilt thou have me to do?' When he had learnt to obey God he was given power under God's authority.

We must learn to obey too, if we later are to have authority over others. For the present you are like the centurion, one *under* authority.

Prayer: Lord Jesus Christ, give us such a love of you that nothing may seem too difficult to do or to suffer in obeying your will, whether it be that found in the Bible, or that imposed upon us by others under your authority. And grant that in thus obeying you we may become more like you in character and in love and power. *Amen.*

3. *How Far are you Going?*

A PARABLE OF STEWARDSHIP

Scripture Reading: Luke 19:11–24.
Key Verse: 13. Occupy till I come.
Hymn: Awake my soul.

Some men were chatting about how far they had travelled in their cars during the past year and soon the discussion got competitive. One said that he had covered 10,000 miles, another said that he had done 12,000, yet another bragged that he had always gone more than 15,000 miles each year that he had had his car and the last one boasted that he had clocked up 19,000 miles that year. The oldest had said nothing for he had never owned a car. One of the company jokingly said to him, 'How many miles have you done?' He replied, 'A million.' Pressed to explain this startling statement he said, 'I have driven an average of seventy miles each day, six days a week; that's over 20,000 miles each year, that's more than any of you, and I've done it foı fifty years.'

Just imagine, a million miles! The London to Sydney car race caused much excitement, but this man had gone as far 160 times, or the equivalent of 1,000 return journeys between London and John o' Groats or Land's End, or forty times round the world, or as far as the astronauts in Apollo eleven and twelve travelled in their two journeys to the moon and back!

What pleasure he must have had driving to the countryside or to seaside resorts! He must have visited them all. But the imagination was spoiled by one of the company saying, 'But you haven't got a car!' He had to explain.

'I drive a brand new car every day straight from our motor factory to the motor sales firms in towns within a radius of seventy miles, mostly to London.'

'Not much fun in that,' said one, 'A bit monotonous and

boring. You never got anywhere really. A million miles to nowhere.'

'No, but it was necessary and useful,' he answered.

Today so many people are out 'to get somewhere' in life; some have been all round the world, or visited scores of countries for pleasure, but have never done anything really useful. They have truly gone far and got nowhere, for they have been of no use to anyone. Our hero had travelled a million miles but every journey had been of real use to someone. Thousands of people had him to thank for the safe delivery of their new cars.

Jesus told the story of a nobleman who was going to a far country to receive a kingdom. Before he went he gave a pound to each of his ten servants and told them, 'Occupy (look after it), till I come.' When he returned he asked each one what he had done with the pound. The one who had done nothing with his pound had it taken away from him, but those who had put their pound to good use were given great rewards.

The pound represents the life that Jesus our creator gave us. He expects us to put it to good use, and when He returns He will reward us according to the amount we have used it. Are you putting your life to good use? Using it for others, not yourself?

Jesus never travelled more than 100 miles from Jerusalem and met His death at the early age of thirty-three on a cross. Would you say that He got nowhere? In those few years He did more good to others than any other person who ever lived, and by His death and resurrection made our journey to heaven possible.

Don't worry how far you are going, but rather how much use you are to others.

Prayer: O God, we thank you for the life you have given us. We pray that we may spend it in the service of others, after the example of Jesus who went about doing good and gave His life for us all. *Amen.*

4. *Twice Mine*

A PARABLE OF GOD'S LOVE

Scripture Reading: 1 Corinthians 6:19, 20.
Key Verse: 20. You are bought with a price.
Hymn: There is a green hill.

Little Tommy saw his friends sailing their boats on the paddling-pool near the sea-front and wished that he had a little yacht of his own. So he asked his father if he would buy him one. His father said, 'You can have one for Christmas.' 'But I want one now,' he replied.

'In that case you'll have to make one. I'll find you a suitable piece of wood and a bit of lead for a keel and I expect that mother will have a spare length of cloth for the sails. I'll show you how to make it, but you'll have to do the work yourself,' his father said.

You can imagine how busy Tommy was for the next couple of weeks. He really took great care over his little yacht, sandpapering it till it was perfectly smooth and trying it in water to see that it was evenly balanced on its keel, and finally painting it so that it shone in the sun. Mother helped him a bit with the sewing of the sails, but he could truly say that he had built it himself. How proud he was when at last the paint was dry and he took it to the pool. Some of his friends were quite envious whilst one said openly, 'I wish I could make a boat like that.'

It sailed so well on the shallow pool that he decided to take it down to the sea. He had learnt how to set the sails so that the boat would sail in a circle and always come back to him, so he did this and the craft behaved perfectly. Every day except Sunday he went to the shore and played proudly with his home-made vessel.

But one day, whilst the boat was on the sea, a strong gust of wind pulled the sail from its fastening and this altered the direction of the boat. Alas for Tommy, the little craft kept sailing out to sea. Tommy cried out but there was no one near to help. He watched it move farther and farther away until at last he could see it no longer. He ran home and told his parents who tried to comfort him, but he had come to love so much what he had made that he didn't get over his loss.

Months later, passing a little general stores, a boat in the window drew his attention. Although it had a 75 new pence price tag on it, it was without doubt, Tommy's own boat. He ran inside and told the shop-keeper his story and asked for his boat back.

'I'm sorry lad,' the man said, 'but a fisherman found this well out to sea and he sold it to me. If you want it you'll have to pay the 50 pence I gave him for it, and that's cheap.'

Tommy was sensible enough to ask the shopkeeper to put it aside for him and ran home as fast as he could to tell his mother. She couldn't help him so he went to his father who listened to his story and then said, 'I'll lend you the 50 pence but you'll have to go without your pocket-money for ten weeks until you've paid me back.' Tommy readily agreed and ran to the shop and bought back his boat. He missed his pocket-money over such a long time, but he thought it was well worth it. 'Now it's twice mine,' he was fond of saying and he never let it get away again.

God is to us what Tommy was to that boat. Genesis 1 reminds us that God made us, and John's gospel reminds us that when we sinned and became lost to God, because He loved us so much He gave up His own Son to buy us back. Paul tells the Corinthians, 'You are bought with a price.' Jesus willingly went to the cross to pay the price of our sins so that we might become God's sons too and live with Him forever.

Prayer: Almighty God, we thank you for creating us and all the blessings you have given us, but most of all for giving Jesus to die for our sins. Make us truly thankful, and help us to show our gratitude by serving you all our lives. *Amen.*

5. *Ask Father*

A PARABLE OF PRAYER

Scripture Reading: Matthew 7:7–11.
Key Verse: 9. What man if his son asks for bread, will give him a stone?
Hymn: Prayer is the soul's sincere desire.

Wolfgang's father was the musical director to the archbishop of Salzburg in Austria. But the pay was poor, so he had to live in a humble cottage near some woods, and teach music to the children of richer parents. Even so the family often went without food. But the father was determined that his children should have as good a musical training as the other boys and girls that he taught. So, at the age of six, Wolfgang's sister could play any tune that she heard upon the harpsichord, an early kind of piano. Wolfgang was even more talented than his sister. At the age of three he knew the names of all the birds he saw and could recognize their songs and play them in little tunes that he made up. All this made for a happy family, but it didn't provide them with enough food.

One day Wolfgang overheard his mother tell his father that they had no bread for the next day, and father said he had no money. He called his sister to go to the woods with him and she readily agreed. They found a grassy bank by the side of the river and sat in the shade of a huge tree.

'Why are you so sad?' Frederica asked, 'You are usually so happy.'

'I heard mother say that there wasn't even any bread left to eat,' Wonfgang replied. 'Let us ask God to send us some bread.'

'But would God send us bread just because we asked for it?' posed Frederica. She didn't get an answer because Wolfgang was already on his knees, and she joined him at once. In simple child-like talk they asked their heavenly Father to send them bread to eat and to help their mother and father. After they said, 'Amen', they sat down again to discuss how they could help.

'One day someone important will hear me play the harpsichord and I shall become famous and play before lots of people and earn lots of money. Then I will buy mother and father a big house, and they will have all the food that they want,' Wolfgang mused.

Suddenly they were startled by a man laughing and saw him emerge from the other side of the great tree-trunk.

'Please don't laugh at my brother,' Frederica said, 'because he really can play lovely music, even though he's only six. If you'll only walk with us to our cottage he will play for you.'

The man said he would come later and asked where the cottage was. That afternoon a very different man came, dressed in a fine uniform and carrying a large hamper full of all kinds of rich foods and drinks. He announced that the man the children had met in the woods would call at eight o'clock that night, and departed. The parents questioned Frederica who explained how they had prayed to God for bread and now he had answered their prayers. They were so excited and after a feast began to prepare for their kind visitor.

Imagine their surprise when Wolfgang's father answered the knock at the door and introduced their visitor as His Imperial Majesty, Francis I. The Emperor had brought other friends with him who understood music better than he did, and when they were all seated Wolfgang went to the harpsichord and began to play. The Emperor didn't need his friends to tell him that Wolfgang had exceptional ability, for it would have been good for a learned adult. The Emperor was not only amazed but very pleased. Humbly he admitted, 'What you said was true, and I will help your dream to play before large audiences to come true too, and you will be known as the musician of musicians.' And this he did.

At thirteen Wolfgang Mozart was made a chevalier or Knight of the Golden Spur by the Pope. He toured many countries and composed much music and is still very famous today.

Wolfgang simply believed Jesus when He said, 'Ask and you shall receive,' so he asked and got more than he asked for.

'If you ask for bread your heavenly Father will not give you a stone, but much better things,' Jesus said.

Let us not forget God, but daily ask Him for our needs.

Prayer: The Lord's Prayer.

6. *Keeping Promises*

A PARABLE OF FAITHFULNESS

Scripture Reading: John 2:13–22.
Key Verse: 22. . . . they believed the word which Jesus said.
Hymn: The Lord's my Shepherd.

Did you know that the great Emperor Napoleon, when a boy, didn't like school dinners? Whilst at the army school at Brienne, he preferred to buy fruit from a barrow just outside the school gates. The girl in charge of the barrow was very popular with the students and Napoleon bought as much fruit as anyone. Sometimes he had no money but the girl would insist that he took the fruit saying that he could pay her back when he could afford it. But the bill grew and grew and by the time that Napoleon left the school to go into the army, he owed far too much to be able to pay it all. He gave the girl what money he had and promised to return and pay later.

As the years went by he became more famous, and his life filled with more important things so the fruit-girl and his debt to her receded from his memory. The battles in which he took part and later his office as Emperor of France with the attendant problems of State, eventually erased from his mind the matter of his promise.

Very many years later, Napoleon chanced to pass through Brienne, and ordered the route to be changed so that he could visit his old school. As he approached the gates and saw a couple of barrow-boys outside, the girl, his debt and his promise returned to his mind, and his conscience too. All thoughts of visiting the school went and in their place was an intense desire to find the maiden who had been so kind to him in his youth and to repay her. Eventually he discovered that she had married, lost her husband in battle, and with her daughter, kept a small stall in the market-place.

Immediately he went there and found her. Keeping his identity secret he asked, 'What's all the commotion about today?'

'Haven't you heard,' the woman replied, 'The Emperor has come back.'

'Come back? When was he here before then?' Napoleon asked.

'When he was a student in the military school,' she replied. 'I used to have a stall outside and the Emperor often bought fruit from me.'

'Did he always pay for it?' the great man queried.

'Of course, he always paid,' she replied as though offended.

'You must have forgotten him as well as his debt to you, just as he forgot his promise to pay you,' he said. As the woman recognized him he went on, 'I am sorry that it has been so long, but let me reimburse you now,' and he gave her several gold coins. She was in tears yet full of joy; the Emperor had kept his promise! Indeed he did more; he built a fine house for her and settled a sum of money on her to keep her and educate her children too.

The truly great always keep their promises. Do you?

After the Flood God promised (Gen. 8:22), 'While the earth remained seedtime and harvest shall not cease,' and they haven't. To Abraham aged 100 and Sarah, his wife, aged ninety, God promised a son, and Isaac was born. To the Children of Israel God promised a land of their own, and they came into Canaan and possessed the land which they still hold today.

Jesus promised (John 2:19), 'Destroy this temple (My body) and in three days I will raise it up again.' They crucified Him, but on the third day He rose from the grave, and in the forty days that followed He was seen by hundreds of people.

Jesus said (John 11:25), 'He that believeth on Me, though he were dead yet shall he live.' (John 14:3) 'I go to prepare a place for you that where I am, there you may be also.' And Jesus was the greatest of all men. He will keep these promises too. If we will believe Him, then one day we will live with Him for ever. Do you?

Prayer: O God, even when we do not fully understand, help us to have faith to believe that you love us, and will keep your promises to care for us and all our needs, both in this world and the next. *Amen.*

7. Follow the Leader

A PARABLE OF DISCIPLESHIP

Scripture Reading: Matthew 4:18–25.
Key Verse: 20. They followed Him.
Hymn: Lead us, heavenly Father, lead us.

Two days before the war began in 1939, the children who lived in large cities were evacuated with their teachers to the countryside where they would be safe from air-raids. My group of fifty London children were taken to Marcham, a village near Abingdon in Berkshire. Things were very strange to the town boys and girls until they got used to them, and then they enjoyed them, like helping with the haymaking, and riding home on the back of a farm horse.

The winter of 1940 was very cold and the ditches and ponds were frozen over. The London boys who had only had a little enjoyment from a home-made slide on a slippery patch on the road in town, found it great fun to have a huge slide provided by nature in the form of the village pond. The local children had skates, but the London children, not to be outdone, tried to copy the various skills of the skaters without the advantage of skates. They ran hard, leapt on to the ice and slid a great distance, first on two feet, then on one foot, then with two knees bent, and finally on one foot with that knee bent and the other leg projecting straight in front. This was called 'Little Man'.

David Neal was only seven years old, but he was not going to be outdone by the older children, so he tried Little Man too. But alas he lost his balance and went sliding across the pond on all fours, face down.

'Now let's see someone copy that', one wag remarked. But it was not a laughing matter, for David's cheek was deeply cut and the little chap was in tears. I rushed him off to Abingdon Hospital where they inserted several stitches.

That evening I went to his foster-parents' house and asked to see David. He had just got into bed. After saying that he felt much better he asked me to tell him a story before he went to sleep.

I told him about a ram, who, one summer, found a gap in a hedge and thought that it would be fun to see what was on the other side of it. He discovered a deep, wide and dry hole which the farmer had dug in the winter to drain off surplus water. He was able to leap to the far edge and scramble to safety. A sheep saw the ram disappear and decided to follow, another sheep followed him and so on. But the sheep were not as agile as the ram, and each one fell into the whole until it was full up and only the last ones were able to escape on the backs of those below, but many were hurt and those at the bottom died.

David was smart enough to realize that I had told the story with a purpose.

'I suppose I was like a silly sheep, following others without stopping to think what might happen to me if I did', he said.

'It's like a game of Follow the Leader, it's only all right if you know that you can trust the leader not to do anything silly or unkind,' I added.

Are you like David was? If we wish to go mountaineering we must have a guide, someone who knows the way, has been there before, and come back, and one on whom we can utterly depend. Life is like climbing a mountain which leads through death to heaven. Jesus is the only one who has been there before and come back, and if we wish to get there safely we must follow Him.

Jesus called to James and John, Andrew and Simon, 'Follow Me.' They were wise and left everything to follow Him. So did many others. If we are wise we shall not be like sheep that go astray, as Isaiah said (53:6), but follow Jesus. He is a leader we can trust to keep us from harm and wrong.

Prayer: May the strength of God pilot us,
The power of God preserve us,
The wisdom of God instruct us,
The hand of God protect us,
And the way of God direct us,
Now and evermore. *Amen.*

8. *The Father's Choice*

A PARABLE OF OBEDIENCE

Scripture Reading: Psalm 47:1–4.
Key Verse: 4. He shall choose our inheritance for us.
Hymn: Dear Lord and Father of mankind.

You must have visited, at some time or other, one of the large stores in town at Christmas time, and gone to the toy and games department and thought how wonderful it would be if someone said you could choose what you liked best to take home. But did it ever happen to you?

It did to one little girl. Her name was Emma and her father was the great American evangelist Dwight Moody. He visited many countries and came to England twice. Thousands flocked to hear him. As he was so often away from home, he liked to take presents back to his wife and daughter. On one occasion, however, he returned without a present for Emma, so he asked her to go to the Toy Store with him to choose one for herself.

You can imagine how excited she was. The store in Chicago sold only toys, so they went to the doll department at Emma's request. There was every possible kind of doll; larger than life dolls, and dolls you could put in a thimble; dolls of every colour and country dressed in their own national costume; rag dolls and china dolls. But the one that caught Emma's eye was a fairy doll, quite the most beautiful doll in the place, dressed in a scintillating dress of shining white, and holding a magic wand in her hand. Emma went round the department twice, but each time she came back to the fairy doll. She had quite made up her mind when she noticed the price on the tag. She didn't want to be greedy, so she looked around a little longer and finally chose a much cheaper doll.

'Is that the one you really want?' asked father who had noticed the long looks she had given the fairy doll.

'Yes, thank you father,' she said. So the money was paid and Emma carried her doll out, trying to forget the fairy doll.

That night when Emma went to bed her father went with her. When she was tucked up comfortably he said to her, 'If I had chosen for you I would have picked the fairy doll.' Emma turned over and tried not to let her father see the tears that were coming to her eyes.

After his next trip away from home, father once more asked Emma if she would like to go with him to choose a present for herself. 'Oh no,' she replied, 'you pick one for me. You always choose best.'

The Psalmist said that God had chosen our inheritance for us. God our heavenly Father always chooses best, and if we are wise we will be content with his choice.

God chose a perfect paradise for Adam to live in, but Adam chose to do what he thought was best and finished up as a farmer in a weed and thistle ridden field outside Eden. Noah, however, chose to do things God's way, and built a boat at God's direction. Everyone, apart from his family, laughed at him when he said he was preparing for a flood, but they were all drowned except Noah and his family. How glad he must have been that he was content with God's choice.

And so it was throughout the history of Israel. When they followed God's choice and obeyed him all went well. When they chose to go their own way, God left them to fend for themselves and things went badly. They were taken from the land God their Father had given them and were captives in a foreign land for seventy years.

God has chosen for us a full abundant life here on earth, and a perfect heaven to live in afterwards. 1 Corinthians 2:9 says, 'Eye hath not seen nor ear heard, neither hath it entered into the heart of man the things that God hath prepared for those that love him.' If we let our heavenly Father choose for us, and go his way, obey him, we shall get what he has chosen for us. The Father's choice is best.

Prayer: O God, our heavenly Father, who love us so much that you call us your children, help us always to follow your choice and not go our own way, so that we may inherit all you have chosen for us, and so glorify your name. *Amen.*

9. *Full Value*

A PARABLE OF BEAUTY

Scripture Reading: Matthew 6:25–34.
Key Verses: 28, 29. Consider the lilies of the field . . .
Hymn: For the beauty of the earth.

When you go to a shop to buy something you like to get full value for your money. Do you get full value of what God has given you for nothing? Take your eyes for example. It is useful to be able to see where you are going, so that you don't bump into things, to enjoy reading a book, to be able to select which sweets you want to buy, and so on. But do you get full value out of your eyes? Do you appreciate the beauty that is all around you?

Joseph Turner, one of our greatest painters, was giving an exhibition of his works when a lady came up to him and said, 'I never see such beautiful clouds and skies as those you have painted.' Turner replied, 'No, madam, but don't you wish you could?' Beauty is there for all to see, but not all see beauty.

One evening, when Lorado Taft, an American sculptor, was entertaining some guests, he invited them on to the veranda to see the sunset. He pointed out the immense variety of colours that there were, yet they never clashed, and how they gradually melted into other shades, a constantly changing panorama. A negro maid, who was collecting empty glasses, overheard and asked her master if she could be excused for ten minutes to run to her mother's house. He asked why. She explained that she wanted to show her mother the sunset. The company laughed. Mr. Taft laughed too.

'Your mother has always lived in this village, and must have seen thousands of sunsets,' he said. The maid was very quick to reply, 'Oh no sir, we never saw any sunsets until you came.'

A science teacher once pointed out some beauty to his class when he placed a blade of grass under a microscope and let them see its beauty of design. One lad remarked, 'I wish you hadn't shown it to me. I shall never want to step on grass again.' He was beginning to have his eyes opened to the full beauty of God's handiwork. The class asked for more, so he put the head of a dandelion weed under the microscope. They saw the beauty of the form of the pollen dust and were told that there are 365,000 grains on each plant. Do you wonder that Jesus, who made all things, pointed out the common poppy and said, 'Consider the lilies of the field, how they grow. They toil not, neither do they spin, yet even Solomon, in all his glory was not arrayed like one of these.' Did you know that every tiny snowflake is different from another, having only six rays as the common basis of its great beauty. Just think how much beauty there is in one snowball that you so lightly gather and smash. God showed that he knew of this beauty when he said to Job, (38:22), 'Hast thou entered into the treasures of the snow, or hast thou seen the treasures of the hail?'

In the East-End of London, during the war, when bombed sites were as common as houses, the ugliness of such devastation was plain for all to see. But as the months went past, grass and weeds, and the magenta-coloured willow-herb in particular, began to clothe the ruins with a beauty which made the people feel that God was healing the ugly wounds that man had made upon his earth. The children were invited to collect the flowers to see how many different kinds there were, and soon began to appreciate their various beauties.

More important than seeing beauty, is being beautiful, and I don't mean false eye-lashes and lipstick. How does one learn to become the kind of person whose beauty shines through the face? It was the wisest of men, King Solomon, who said, (Proverbs 23:7), 'As he thinketh in his heart, so is he.' Glenn Clark, who lived so close to God that his every prayer was answered affirmatively, put this thought another way, 'You become what you adore.' If we gaze at beautiful things long enough and often enough, we shall begin to recognize beauty and become more beautiful in our lives. Paul, inspired by God's Holy Spirit said (Philippians 4:8), 'Whatsoever things are lovely, think on these things.' Think more about the beauty of Jesus' life, and become more like Him.

Prayer: We thank you, Lord Jesus Christ, for the beauties of the earth and the glories of the sky, the blossoms of flowers and the colours of birds, the shapes of trees and the splendour of the hills. In all that you have made we see the wonder of your love and care. Help us always to trust this love which is beyond our understanding, yet continues to surround our lives with beauty, so that we may grow more like you. *Amen.*

10. Fellow-Workers

A PARABLE OF CHOICE

Scripture Reading: 1 Corinthians 3:6–11.
Key Verse: 9. Labourers together with God.
Hymn: Breathe on me breath of God.

Eight hundred years ago, at the court of King Henry I of England, things were gay. There were pageants and feasts in plenty and much merry-making. Most of the fun was provided by the court jester in a red habit, pointed shoes and a cap with bells. He was a great favourite but this life brought him no real satisfaction. Behind his mask of gaiety was a heart full of sorrow for the poor and needy.

When the king's eldest son was drowned at sea in the White Ship, sadness came to the whole court, and Rahere, the jester, was not required. So he took this opportunity to go on a pilgrimage to Rome during which time he hoped he would be guided to find some work which would be of some help to God and his fellow men. The journey was dangerous for many brigands were abroad, and packs of hungry wolves frequented the roads between towns. Having overcome these hazards he arrived in Rome only to catch the plague which was raging.

Alone in a room deserted by his landlord since his illness, he felt at the point of death. He wanted so much to live to do something really useful that he prayed that if God would restore him he would spend the rest of his life in God's service, doing something to help sick people in England.

God heard this prayer and answered it. Gradually he got better and his first outing was to the near-by church of St. Bartholomew in Rome, to thank God and ask for His guidance. That night, in a dream, a large man came to him and introduced himself as St. Bartholomew. 'I have been sent by God to help you,' he said. 'On your return to

London you must knock at the door of the king's chamber. It will be opened to you. You must seek for a place called the Smooth Field in London and you will find it. Upon your admittance to the king's presence you must ask for the Smooth Field and it will be given to you. There you will build a church, a priory and a hospital. Do not fear for I will see that you get all the money and the help you need!'

Changing his clothes to that of a humble friar, he returned to London. On arrival he soon found the flat marshy area called Smooth Field, used only by horse dealers as a market-place, and the public hangman. The gallows stood there. Then he made haste for the anteroom to the king's chamber.

In a simple brown robe tied with rope, and with a serious face, the jester was not recognized at first. On giving his name however, he was admitted. The king was pleased to see him, and after hearing Rahere's full story he granted him the Smooth Field without question.

The following morning Rahere was down at the Smooth Field very early and soon made friends with the children playing there. They thought it a great game collecting the stones and digging trenches to drain the marshy parts. They told their parents what they had been doing and soon the parents were lending a hand. Courtiers who knew Rahere came to laugh but didn't depart without leaving some gold to help the plan. The horse dealers also offered money in lieu of rent, and so gradually the church was built, followed by the priory, and at last Rahere's great desire, the hospital was completed, the first in England. It was named St. Bartholomew's hospital, of course, though today it is St. Bart's, for short, in what is now called Smithfield. Other hospitals grew up all over the country in the years that followed. Millions of people have visited St. Bart's in the past 800 years, and found health, thanks to Rahere the little jester who gave up merry-making to join hands with God for work of a more serious and useful kind.

It may be more fun to become a famous entertainer than a social-worker, a preacher, a teacher or a builder of hospitals, but the most abiding work we do is that which we do with God's help and guidance. Alone there is little we can do. With God there is nothing that we cannot do.

Prayer: Grant to us, O Lord, the desire to think and do always those things that please you, so that we can, by you be enabled to live and work with your guidance, and according to your will. *Amen.*

11. *Sir Francis Chantrey*

A PARABLE OF CONTENTMENT

Scripture Reading: 1 Timothy 6:5–12.
Key Verse: 6. Godliness with contentment is great gain.
Hymn: We thank you, Lord of heaven.

Little Francis Chantrey loved to stare. As a baby he would stare at his mother and follow her with his eyes whenever she was in the room. As he grew up he would stare at a flower or a tree until his parents grew impatient and told him to 'Come along'. Most of all he loved to look at animals, especially young ones. He would play contentedly for hours with his kitten and attempts to distract him with offers of sweets never succeeded. In 1790 when the family moved from Derbyshire to the village of Norton, near the town of Sheffield, his father bought a donkey for travelling to and from the town. Francis would watch him every step of the way. At night he would sketch him in all kinds of positions, and because he had watched him so carefully the drawings were very good. He did the same with his other animals, the cat and the pig. When other children called him to play with them he would go, but he soon grew tired of their games and returned to his animals, his painting and modelling.

One day a visitor came to the house and accepted an invitation to stay to dinner. Mrs. Chantrey made a large meat pie. As there was quite a lot of dough left, Francis asked if he could have it. She said he could, so he gleefully took it away and made it into little cats and pigs and donkeys. His mother decorated the pie with them. You can imagine the visitor's surprise when he saw the splendid pie. 'I do declare, ma'am', he said, 'I have never seen a more magnificent pie. It seems a shame to eat it. Where did you buy it?'

'We couldn't afford to buy a pie,' she said, 'I made it and Francis formed the animals. He is always drawing and modelling. He seems to see beauty in so many things that we don't.'

The gentleman commented, 'That is why he does it so well. One day he will become a famous sculptor and become rich if he is given the chance.'

'I don't care about money, sir, or about being famous,' Francis replied, 'I am content to make beautiful things.'

When his father died Francis had to start work to earn money, though he was only twelve. He found a shop in town which sold paintings and other works of art. When the owner saw Francis' paintings and carvings he was glad to give him work. There, in Sheffield, he learned to paint portraits, and the money he earned by the time he was a young man, enabled him to move to London. He rented a little attic and lived frugally, but he was happy making his little carvings, and soon began to be visited by famous artists and sculptors. They helped him and soon he was carving life-size models and began to work in stone. As the horses and dogs and people began to form under his hands he was full of joy at being able to produce such beautiful work for all to see.

As the years went by he did become very famous. He made statues of George III and George IV and was knighted and statues he made of other famous men are to be found in the British Museum, Westminster Abbey, Lichfield Cathedral and other well-known places. All this made him rich too. But he was satisfied with making beauty for all to enjoy.

When he died he left well over £100,000 to the Royal Academy to buy works of art for the nation. If you go to the Tate Gallery in London for instance, you will see two hundred paintings with the words 'Chantrey Bequest'. So even after his death there is much beauty for us to take pleasure in, thanks to little Francis who didn't seek fame or money but was content with the joy of beautiful things.

As Paul said to young Timothy, 'Love of money is the root

of all evil, but godliness with contentment is great gain.' Be content with what God has given you and make the most of it.

Prayer: O God, who has given us so many good and beautiful things in this world, we thank you for all your blessings and ask only that you will give us contented minds, so that we may be willing to give our talents and spend our lives for the joy of others, even as your Son, Jesus did. *Amen.*

12. Without Wax

A PARABLE OF SINCERITY

Scripture Reading: Joshua 24:13–18.
Key Verse: 14. . . . serve the Lord in sincerity and truth.
Hymn: Awake my soul and with the sun.

In these days when money seems to be worth less each year, when the cost of things keeps going up yet the articles we buy seem to be of poorer quality than they used to be, many people are investing their money in buying antiques because the value of these keeps increasing. But it is easy to be deceived so they take an expert with them to be sure of getting a genuine article. Some dealers have been known to take an old piece of china or furniture which has been broken and mend it carefully so that it might not be noticed and sell it at the price of a perfect antique.

'When the Romans conquered most of the known world they often brought back beautiful objects of art from the lands that they had conquered, like vases or statues from Greece. Later quite a trade in statues sprang up between these two countries. Most of the statues were flawless, but occasionally some sculptors would hit too hard and a crack would appear, spoiling the work. A life-size piece of stone cost a great deal of money and the artists couldn't afford such waste, so they mixed some fine powder from the stone with some wax, and then filled the crack with this kind of cement. When it dried the crack couldn't be seen. The statues were then sold as perfect. But as the months went by the hot weather began to melt the wax and the cracks became visible. Naturally the Romans felt that they had been cheated. To avoid this the Greek sculptors were made to produce a letter guaranteeing that their work was 'without wax', or in Latin, 'sine cera', or as we say today, 'sincere'.

Bonnie Prince Charlie wasn't the only 'Pretender'. Jacob

pretended that he was Esau to get his father's blessing; Sarah pretended that she wasn't Abram's wife to gain favour with the Egyptians; Peter pretended he never knew Jesus when his Master was arrested; Judas pretended he was a faithful disciple of Jesus' when he betrayed Him to the soldiers; Ananias pretended that he had given all the proceeds of the sale of his house and land when he had kept back some part of it. Are you a pretender? Do you truly mean all the things you sing in your hymns? One hymn says that 'prayer is the soul's sincere desire'. Do you really mean all you say in your prayers? And this should apply to other people as well as to God. Are you sincere, true, frank and straightforward in all you say and do?

Jesus was perfectly sincere at all times. Before the common people or before the Jewish leaders, He was just the same, absolutely true. He told Pilate no lies and He refused to pretend in His answers to the Council of the Sanhedrin, though He knew such sincerity would cost Him agony and death.

We should catch this spirit of sincerity if we are to go on calling ourselves Christians. Are we genuine, real all through like Jesus? In our Bible story today Joshua was telling his people not to pretend. In travelling from slavery in Egypt to the Promised Land they had mixed with many foreigners and some had started to worship other gods, yet they continued to accept all the blessings the God of Israel gave them. 'Stop pretending,' he says, 'If you want to serve other gods be open about it. You must choose today whom you are going to serve. But if you choose to serve the God of Israel who has been with us since we began this journey and has brought us safely into this land of grapes and olives, then you must serve him in sincerity and in truth.' This was Joshua's last address to his people, and he was sincere, he meant every word he said. Israel's only hope was in serving the Lord truly and not pretending. Paul says that it is absolutely essential to be sincere in our love for God.

We too must serve God and honour Him in sincerity and truth.

Prayer: Lord Jesus we want to be honest and true and sincere in all we say to you and to others. Please put your spirit within us so that we shall be able to overcome the temptation to pretend and all our speech and action may be open and frank and true. Help us to admit our wrong and accept fair blame. In Jesus' Name we ask it. *Amen.*

13. A Fruit of the Spirit

A PARABLE OF SELF-CONTROL

Scripture Reading: 1 Samuel 24.
Key Verse: 18. When the Lord had delivered me into thine hand thou killedst me not.
Galatians 5:23. A fruit of the spirit is self-control.
Hymn: Heavenly Father, may thy blessing.

Fighting broke out on the terraces at Highbury. A little supporter of the Arsenal F.C. got into an argument with a bigger Chelsea fan and their tempers got hotter and hotter until a fight started. The little chap got the worst of it. Do you think that because the Chelsea supporter won the fight it proved that the Chelsea team were better players than the Arsenal men? All the fight proved was that neither of the two boys knew how to control himself. Can you control yourself? Listen to this story of a man who won a fight, put yourself in his place and ask yourself if you would have acted as he did?

Louis XII of France was much loved by his people and was known best, not as king, but as father of his country. He was indeed, very kind to all, even his enemies.

He spent some years conducting battles in the north of Italy, and because he was a good soldier, won a great deal of territory. He conquered the town of Agnadel in 1509, and a Venetian general was captured. The well-mannered Louis accorded the vanquished general the honour due to one of his rank, treating him almost as a friend. Upon promising not to run away, he was given freedom to roam the town unmolested and the French soldiers were ordered to salute him and afford him every courtesy. But the general who would have imprisoned Louis if their positions had been reversed, looked upon Louis' chivalry as weakness and began to insult him before the soldiers. Soon he began to give them orders and became abusive when these were referred to the king before being obeyed.

Officers protested to Louis and the general was called to the king's presence and his ungallant conduct reprimanded. Instead of apologizing, the general became enraged. This was too much for even the patient Louis who abruptly commanded, 'Take him outside the city and set him free before I lose my temper and have him incarcerated in a dungeon. It is more important to conquer myself than to conquer him.' Was this weakness or wisdom?

In the Bible Joseph was sold into slavery in Egypt by his brothers, but this led to his becoming the most important man in the country after Pharaoh himself. When his brothers came to Egypt for corn during a famine, they were brought before him. Did he vent his spite on them? No, he forgave them and held a party and sent for the father to come and join them in the luxury of the Egyptian court. Joseph knew the great value of self-control.

When king Saul was trying to catch young David to kill him because he had heard that he was to be the next king, David hid in a cave. Whilst the hunt was on, Saul unsuspectingly entered this cave to rest. David could have killed Saul then but he would not. He merely cut off a piece of the king's robe which he showed to him later to prove that he had spared Saul's life. But this did not stop Saul making other efforts to capture David and was more than once beside himself with rage at his failures. Eventually he was killed at Gilboa in a battle against the Philistines and David became king. God rewards those who exercise self-control. Before you are given control of others you must learn to control yourself.

Jesus must have learnt this lesson well for although He did no wrong, when the temple soldiers came to arrest Him and His disciples produced two swords to defend Him, He told them to put them away, and He healed the ear of the soldier who had been hurt in the affray. He showed self-control again when the Council of the Sanhedrin accused Him falsely, but most of all when they crucified Him. Paul says to be temperate, that is to have self-control, is to have the Spirit of Jesus.

Prayer: Lord Jesus Christ, we ask you to help us this day to do nothing for which we will be sorry. Put your Holy Spirit within us so we shall be courteous and forbearing to any who offend us. Give us strength to control our tempers at all times, through Jesus Christ Our Lord. *Amen.*

14. Bother Adam!

A PARABLE OF TEMPTATION

Scripture Reading: Luke 4:1–14.
Key Verse: Mat. 6:13. Lead us not into temptation but deliver us from evil.
Hymn: O Jesus, I have promised.

When our town school was evacuated two days before war broke out, many of the children were looking forward to the chance of a prolonged stay in the countryside, of which they had little experience. They weren't disappointed either. There was much that was new to see and a lot of fun to be had helping with the haymaking or skating on icy ponds. There was a great deal that we learned too. I thought that I knew my Bible well until I met the ploughman George Stimpson. It was one evening whilst out with two boys, Tom and Roger, that we saw old George tending his vegetable patch near his cottage. He was down on his hands and knees picking stinging-nettles from among the carrots. Each time he got to the end of a row he would straighten his back, mop his brow with a red handkerchief and remark, 'Bother Adam.' 'Adam who?' Tom asked. 'Just Adam,' he replied, 'He didn't have another name.' Then I realized that he was referring to the first man on earth. 'But why does he bother you?' I queried. I didn't expect the reply that I got.

'Don't you know your Bible? If it wasn't for Adam giving way to temptation and eating the one forbidden fruit in the garden of Eden, I wouldn't have to break my back weeding day after day.' Then I remembered. It was because of this first sin that God sent Adam out to work by the sweat of his brow and only then that thistles and thorns and weeds began to grow. I explained this to the boys.

'You would have thought that he would have been

content with an abundance of fruit and not touched the one tree that was forbidden,' said Roger. If you had been in Adam's place would you have rejected the temptation? Do you agree with Roger? I told this story to the vicar with whom I was staying. He laughed but said nothing.

Months later the vicar invited Tom and Roger back to tea after Sunday School. They came. Their eyes nearly popped out of their heads. The large dining-table was crowded with good things to eat, sandwiches, buns, jellies, trifles, crumpets, tarts, creamy cakes and éclairs. Right in the middle was a very large plate with a huge dish cover over it. The vicar said grace and then invited us to tuck in.

'Help yourselves to whatever you like,' he said, 'but don't touch the covered dish in the middle. It isn't good for you and you wouldn't enjoy it.'

The boys didn't need telling twice. They ate and ate and went on long after I had finished. At this point the vicar got up and asked me if I would take a turn round the garden with him. I agreed and we left the boys to continue their meal. In two minutes we were back and oh! what a mess! It looked as though Tom and Roger had had a pillow-fight. There were feathers everywhere, on tarts, cream cakes, trifles and jellies and all over the floor. The boys were almost in tears but the vicar roared with laughter.

'Who was it that said if he had been in the Garden of Eden, he would have been satisfied with the fruit he was allowed to eat and not touched the forbidden tree?' he asked. Then the boys understood. The vicar had filled the dish-cover with tiny feathers, so that when they couldn't resist the temptation to see what was under the cover, the feathers would fly out and give them away. They were as bad as Adam.

It isn't easy to overcome temptation. Jesus is the only one who never yielded. He had forty days of it and the devil did his worst, but He won through because He was filled with God's Holy Spirit, knew the scriptures perfectly and spent much time in prayer. This is the answer. Jesus said to His disciples when they fell asleep on guard, 'Watch and pray that you don't fall into temptation.' He also taught them to pray, 'Lead us not into temptation but deliver us from evil.' Today will bring its temptations, so let us pray for help.

Prayer: O Lord you know the temptations that come to us. Provide for us a way of escape or empower us to overcome by your Holy Spirit. Help us to do what our consciences tell us is right and at the end grant us the joy you have promised to those who overcome, through Jesus Christ Our Lord. *Amen.*

15. Self-Bound

A PARABLE OF FREEDOM

Scripture Reading: John 8:23–36.
Key Verses: 34. Whoever commits sin is the servant of sin.
36. If the Son shall make you free, you shall be free indeed.
Hymn: Hark! the glad sound.

In the days before rifles and guns, the main weapons of warfare were swords and bows and arrows, and often success in a battle depended upon the strength of the bows and swords. The person who made these was therefore very important. In the days of the early French wars, Louis the Strong was such a one. It was said that no sword or bow of his making had ever been broken. This gave the warriors great confidence in battle.

In one successful conflict the French took many prisoners; so many in fact, that there were not nearly enough cells in the prison to accommodate them all, and many had to be left free to roam in the courtyard under watchful guards. The govenor of the prison thought hard to find a way of holding them safely. Then he remembered Louis the Strong and sent for him. After explaining the situation he asked, 'Can you make me some strong chains and fetters that the prisoners will not be able to break?' 'I have not made many chains, but I know how. I have some good metal and a secret process for tempering, so I can promise to do what you ask,' Louis replied. A contract was signed. Each chain as it was completed was taken to the prison and put to use. They proved so effective that all old chains were replaced by Louis' indestructible ones. So not one man escaped.

Louis' fame as a chainmaker spread to other countries and he made chains for them too. But one of these countries was at war with France and so Louis was put in prison. When he looked at the chains and manacles that bound him he exclaimed, 'I shall never escape from these bonds, for I recognize them as of my own making. I wish I hadn't forged them so well.'

Let us make sure that we don't do the same sort of thing, making a chain to bind ourselves. It is so easy to do. If we persist in our little sins and bad habits, they will get such a hold on us that of our own strength we shall not be able to break free. What a pitiful sight is a 'meths' drinker, or a drug addict in the agony of 'cold turkey', when he will do anything, commit any crime to get more money to buy more drugs or methylated spirit. And it all begins with the first taste, so seemingly harmless.

A boy living in the East-end of London used to go to Sunday School at Bow Church. One Sunday some boys ragged him about going and dared him to go with them instead. Afraid of being called 'chicken', he went. They did some daring things and so he went with them the following Sunday, even though it meant lying to his parents. Soon he was laughing at others who went to church, and learned to steal without being caught. By the time he was twenty he had joined a gang who burgled houses for a living. It became his way of life too.

One Friday they planned to rob the Palace Cinema opposite to Bow Church. The manager had been watched and his movements timed. They knew that the week's takings would be there on the Friday, and that the manager did his round of the cinema at 9 o'clock. As soon as he left his office they entered, stole the money and were about to leave when the manager unexpectedly returned. A short fight ensued in which he was hit a very heavy blow. Then they ran away with the cash. Unfortunately for them, after a short statement to the police, the manager died from the blow. They were caught, convicted and sentenced to life-imprisonment. For that lad it all began with playing the hop from Sunday School; then came lying, stealing, and finally murder. Link by link he had made the chain which bound him for life. So can we. This is what Jesus meant when He said, 'He who commits sin becomes bound by sin.' But there is One who can set us free. God set Shadrach, Meshach and Abed-nego free after they had been bound and thrown into a fierce furnace. He set Peter free of his bonds in prison and led him out. Isaiah said that when Jesus came it would be 'to bring liberty to the captives and the opening of prison to them that are bound.' Have you begun to forge the chain that will bind you? Ask Jesus to set you free. 'If the Son of God sets you free, you will be truly free, once for all.

Prayer: O God we confess it is difficult to break free of the sins with which we have bound ourselves. Please free us through the merits of Jesus Christ our Lord. *Amen.*

16. Unrecognized Value

A PARABLE OF CHRISTMAS

Scripture Reading: John 1:1–14.
Key Verses: 11, 12. He came unto his own but his own received him not. But as many as received him to them gave he power to become the sons of God.
Hymn: O little town of Bethlehem.

The festivities were forgotten that first Christmas of the war. Hitler's Luftwaffe had been bombing London every night, and each morning showed the devastation they had caused. Preservation of life was uppermost in everyone's mind. Parents whose work prevented them from leaving town decided that at least they could send their children to safety in the country. Some children were too small to be sent on their own, but the social and welfare workers were equal to the task.

So it was that on that Christmas Eve, twenty children aged from five down to a baby of one year, arrived at a small village in Berkshire where there were known to be willing foster-parents. The receiving officer welcomed the helpers and the children in the Church Hall, where warm milk and hot cocoa soon warmed the chilly bodies. The foster-mothers had quickly chosen the evacuee they preferred to give a home to, but coloured baby Kenny, crying in his little pram, no one seemed to want. Gradually the hall emptied until only the receiving officer, the helper and tiny Kenny were left.

'There's one lady, Maggie Morland, who didn't come tonight,' the organizer said. 'She has a house full already, but she has a kind heart and may find room for Kenny.' So off they went to Maggie's cottage and knocked.

'Not another,' said Maggie as she opened the door, 'I already have more than I can cope with,' but when she saw the stain of tears on Kenny's cheeks, and his tight black, curly hair, she just couldn't refuse him. 'I suppose he won't take up much room, seeing he's so small,' she said as she picked him out of his pram and cuddled him to her warm bosom. Kenny had found a good home.

Once the bigger children had been packed off to bed, Maggie put a small tin bath before the fire, poured in some warm water, and then proceeded to undress Kenny for his bath. What a surprise she had then! An envelope was attached to Kenny's undervest. Maggie read the words on the outside of the envelope, 'This is for the lady who is kind enough to give my baby a home,' and inside was a note with the address of the coloured parents, and fifty pounds! Maggie was moved to tears. She had never had so much money.

Of course, she told her neighbours, and there were many foster-mothers who wished then that they had chosen Kenny. They would have if they had known what he had to offer. But Maggie who had received him got her biggest present ever.

You remember the story of the first Christmas when baby Jesus wasn't welcome in Bethlehem because no one recognized what He had to offer. As he grew up some accepted Him, but the majority turned on Him in the end and nailed Him to a wooden cross to get rid of Him. But those who believed Jesus to be God's Son come to earth in the flesh, and received Him into their lives, were rewarded with a place in His heavenly kingdom.

Will you recognize Jesus for who He truly is? For those who do, eternal life with Him is their great reward.

'His own didn't receive Him, but those who did believe in Him were privileged to become God's sons.'

Prayer: O God, who at this season of the year, permitted Jesus to become the Son of Man so that we might become the sons of God, help us to recognize the greatness of your gift, and to make room for Christ in our lives, so that we may finally be adopted into your heavenly family. *Amen.*

17. Man's Giant Leap

A PARABLE OF ACENSION DAY

Scripture Reading: Acts 1:1–12.
Key Verse: 11. This same Jesus which is taken up from you into heaven shall so come in like manner.
Hymn: The head that once was crowned with thorns.

What is your greatest leap, your record for the long jump or high jump? When I asked one class this question, a bright spark of a lad said, 'Thirty feet, sir,' and after a pause he added, 'I jumped off the high diving board.' We all laughed and I explained that he was using gravity to assist his leap, whereas the usual jump has to be made against gravity.

Do you keep records of your own achievements? I hope that you do, whatever your sport, because it is better to keep beating your own record than that of someone else. But it is good also to look at world records. What do you consider is the biggest leap anyone has ever made?

1969 will be remembered as the year man set his foot on the moon for the first time. It was Neil Armstrong, the American astronaut who did this. As he stepped from the last rung of the ladder on to the moon he said, 'That's a small step for me but a giant leap for mankind.'

Of course, President Nixon was very pleased. In a speech that was televised to the whole world, he said that he considered man's leap to the moon as the greatest event in human history. But he was wrong. Can you think of a greater leap? Today's Bible reading should give you a clue. Yes, Ascension Day, the day when Jesus left the earth to return to heaven. And He didn't use a booster. He overcame gravity with the power of the Holy Spirit that was in Him. Surely this was a greater event than man reaching the moon.

The same power helped Him to make two other great steps. The first was from heaven to earth at the first Christmas when God took upon Himself human flesh, and the second at the first Easter when Jesus stepped out of the tomb. Aren't these greater events than landing on the moon? God becoming man and man rising from the dead? Remember both these events were witnessed by many people, at least 500 saw His risen form and ascension to heaven.

All these three can be experienced in our lives. We can be born again and made new creatures by believing Christ to be God. We can be resurrected from a dead life to a new life in Christ. Drug addicts, fed up with life, bury themselves in a make-believe world and emerge from their drugs more disillusioned than before. Many of these have found a full, abundantly satisfying life trusting Christ. Others bury themselves in sport. Ted Dexter, one time England's cricket captain, said that he found no solution to life's problems until he put his trust in Christ in June 1969. He advised teenagers to find real life in Christ and to do it in half the time that it took him.

Our reading reminds us that Jesus has another great step to take. The angel at his ascension said, 'This same Jesus which is taken up from you into heaven, shall come again . . .' When He does, He has promised to take all who believe in Him back to heaven with Him. If you believe Christ to be God's Son, then you will one day take a bigger leap, without rocket or space ship, than man has ever done or even imagined. You will ascend as Jesus did to spend eternity with Him.

When small Charles Conrad landed on the moon in the Apollo that followed Neil Armstrong's trip, he joked about Neil's height compared with his, saying, 'It may be a small step for Neil but it's a big one for me.' It may be a small step of faith for some to believe in Jesus Christ, but a big one for you. The important point is, big or small, that you take it. Your ascension depends upon it. Leap now.

Prayer: O God, you have received your Son Jesus Christ into heaven with great glory. Help us to trust in Him now and always, and finally, by the help of your Holy Spirit may we ascend into the place He has prepared for us. *Amen.*

18. The Altar and the Plough

A PARABLE OF HUMILITY

Scripture Reading: John 13:1–17.
Key Verse: 3. Jesus knowing that He was come from God and went to God . . . took a towel and girded Himself.
Hymn: New every morning is the love.

Some of the less able boys in school decided to set the rest an example. They weren't very good at singing or Bible reading, or making up prayers, and they felt that there was more to being a Christian than just worship anyway, so they decided to do something practical. They suggested to the Building Master that they could paint and plaster and paperhang reasonably well and they wanted to do that for God. The local Children's Moral Welfare Committee ran a club to help poor children, but the rooms they had were in a bad condition and discouraged many from going there. The Master suggested that they could redecorate these rooms. Gladly they set to work. Old wallpaper was removed, plaster made good, doors, window-frames and wainscots sanded and the floors and ceilings washed down. Within a week woodwork was being painted, and ceilings and floors made to look almost new, and walls being papered.

The boys did all this themselves and the Master did nothing. Nothing important that is. He cleaned the brushes, made the paste, wiped up drips of paint on the floor, and collected strips of sticky wallpaper as they were trimmed. The menial tasks, the jobs nobody wanted to do, the lowliest work, he took upon himself, although he was the Master. The boys received the praise they truly deserved. Only a few, apart from God, recognized the beauty and humility of the Master's share.

This is what I liked about our reading this morning,

'Jesus knowing that He was come from God and went to God . . . took a towel.' He knew that He was God the Father's Son, and that He was going to return to sit at the Father's right hand, yet He put a towel around His waist, took a basin of water and began to wash the disciples' feet, the task of the lowest servant in a household, and a not very pleasant one. None of the disciples wanted the job, so Jesus did it. Peter felt guilty then and I expect all the others did too. At the end Jesus said, 'You call Me Master and Lord . . . if I then your Lord and Master have washed your feet, you ought to wash one another's feet. This is an example which will make you happy if you copy it. Be humble.'

The Romans had on one of their coins the shape of an ox standing between a plough and an altar. Words below said, 'Ready for either,' ready to serve, to do the normal, daily, useful work, but also ready to do God's work, to be sacrificed if necessary. This is the true meaning of humility. It was true of Jesus in a unique way: as God's Son He was the only one who could pay the price of our sins. We are called to worship God and it means more than hymns and prayers, though these are a necessary part of worship. For us, it may not mean martyrdom but it does mean living as Jesus did, doing good for others, and it especially means being willing to do the humblest tasks.

Florence Nightingale became famous for starting the nursing profession, but it meant, high-born lady that she was, getting down on her knees and scrubbing filthy hospital floors. Sir Wilfrid Grenfell left the prospect of a profitable career in England to serve the seal-fishers and Eskimos of Labrador, with their primitive way of life. Albert Schweitzer, with a doctorate in three different subjects, left everything to serve the lepers of Lambarene, in French Equatorial Africa. These were true Christians showing the humility of Christ. Their own wealth or position or breeding or high mental ability meant nothing to them compared to the desire to serve God and man.

But Christ's greatest act of humility is best stated in the letter Paul wrote to the Philippians, chapter 2, verse 5, 'Let this mind be in you, which was also in Christ Jesus, who, being in the form of God, thought it not robbery to be equal with God: but made Himself of no reputation, and took upon Him the form of a servant, and was made in the likeness of men . . . and humbled Himself, and became obedient unto death . . .' If we would be a Master, we must learn to serve humbly, even if it means a sacrifice.

Prayer: O God, give us the mind and spirit of Christ, that we may be willing to serve all men, no matter how humble the task to which you may call us in your service. *Amen.*

19. Hands

A PARABLE OF PALM SUNDAY

Scripture Reading: Mark 11:1–11.
Key Verse: 2. A colt tied, whereon never man sat.
Hymn: All glory, laud and honour.

An itinerant preacher was travelling through the middle-west states in America. When he came to a ranch where the cowboys were resting after their lunch, he asked them for a drink. They gladly gave him some of their coffee and they got into conversation. They asked why he was in that part of the country and how he earned his living. He explained his mission and soon they were asking questions. One asked if Jesus was truly the Messiah, God's own Son. The preacher reminded him that the following Sunday, Christians the world over would celebrate Palm Sunday, the day on which Christ rode into Jerusalem on an ass, and all the people saw in this the fulfilment of Zechariah's prophecy, that the Jews' Deliverer, the Messiah, would come in this fashion. The preacher took his Bible and read the passage that we read this morning.

When they had almost finished discussing this matter one cowboy said something quite different.

'He must have had wonderful hands,' he said and went on, 'Didn't you say that the colt that Jesus rode on had never been ridden before? We cowboys know how difficult it is to ride an unbroken animal for the first time. It is new to the creature and it makes him afraid, so he rears and bucks to shake his rider off. Sometimes horses that have been broken in by one man won't let another man get on his back, though most animals sense by the rider's touch whether he is friend or foe. I suppose that something like this must have happened that first Palm Sunday, for in spite of the colt being unbroken, and the noise of the people shouting, and the waving of palm branches, the animal appears to have been calm and willing for Jesus to ride him. Something in Jesus' hands or in His touch must have made the creature feel safe and happy and obedient.'

The cowboy was right of course. Jesus did have wonderful hands. They made madmen calm and sane at a touch. They made lame people walk and blind people see. The lepers who nobody would touch for fear of contracting the deadly disease, and were driven away with sticks and stones by most people, were not afraid to come to Jesus. They came right up to Him and He laid His hands on them and they were healed. When He touched the dead body of Jairus' daughter she came back to life. How do you use your hands?

There are doctors and nurses who today are using their hands to make sick people well and skilled surgeons whose hands are vitally important. Red Cross and St. John's Ambulance workers also use their hands to help save life. Almost as important are those who use their hands to make safety equipment or Safety First signs to prevent accidents. What do you use your hands for? Do you do good with them or evil? Do you use them to hurt or to help other children?

Jesus illustrated this in the story of the Good Samaritan, who was so kind to the traveller who had been beaten and robbed and left almost dead. The Samaritan's hands tended the wounds and bound them and set the injured man on his beast. Then he took him to hospital. Use your hands to do good.

Let us not forget that those wonderful hands of Jesus that calmed the foal of an ass, in less than one week were being meekly and willingly stretched out for soldiers to nail to a wooden cross. They were even more wonderful hands then. He let them be used in this cruel way so that we might not have to suffer for our sins. This day you will use your hands many times. For good or for evil? It all depends on you.

Prayer: Almighty God, as today we remember how the people received your Son Jesus Christ into their city in triumph, we ask that we may be willing to accept Him into the citadel of our hearts so that He might triumph there. So may He help us to use our hands not to hinder or hurt, but to help and heal. *Amen.*

20. *Lincoln Cathedral*

A PARABLE OF GIVING

Scripture Reading: Mark 12:41–44.
Key verse: 44. She of her want did cast in all that she had.
Hymn: When I survey the wondrous cross.

Eight hundred years ago a little boy named Hugh, son of the Lord of Avalon, lived in France, and life was full and gay. But sorrow struck the house when he was only eight with the death of his mother. The Lord was heart-broken and sought consolation in a monastery, and Hugh went with him. The monks were kind to him and he enjoyed working in the fields with them, but most of all he loved the peace of the monastery, the stories of Jesus and the deep harmony of the singing at times of worship. When a young man he moved to the Grand Chartreuse and became a monk himself.

Henry II, King of England, who was looking for a new prior to establish a Carthusian monastery at Witham in Somerset, was advised to invite Hugh as he was such a good worker and devout man. The challenge of building a new monastery moved him to accept, but the local people were suspicious of a Frenchman, so he began the work without any help. As the folk got to know him they admired his gentle nature and then began to lend a hand with the building, and also made gifts of money and materials. The priory he built has largely gone now, but the chapel still remains and is part of the parish church.

Hugh didn't stay at Witham very long after this. The news of his good work had reached the king and Hugh was appointed Bishop of Lincoln. Once more he made many friends of the poor with whom he often shared his lunch; he also defended them successfully when they were unjustly taken to the Law Court. He uncovered bribery in high places and made many reforms which stopped corrupt men gaining influential posts where they could rob the poor. When the royal foresters punished peasants who stole the king's deer because they were starving, Hugh took the matter to the king himself and the peasants were freed.

The people were so grateful for all that Hugh had done for them that they pledged their help when he told them of his intention to build a cathedral. The Bishop was wealthy as his father had left him all his money and lands, and this he gladly gave to the building expenses. Such generosity caused even the poorest to give as much as they could afford to help the work.

A poor man who looked after a farmer's pigs came to the Bishop one day and emptied his little cloth bag on a table. There were many coins, though all of low value, and they didn't amount to many all told. But Hugh knew that this man had lived in poverty and had gone hungry many times and had saved every possible penny for a long time to collect this amount. He had given all that he possessed.

The cathedral that Hugh built at Lincoln still stands. The Bishop saw to it that on one pinnacle was a carving of the swineherd for his sacrificial giving. Others arranged for Hugh to be similarly immortalized in stone on another pinnacle for he too had given his all. You can see them both today.

Jesus commended the poor widow who, though she put less in the offering than anyone else, put in all that she had. This is the way the church of Christ has grown. Not by little gifts from people who can well afford it, but by many people giving their all, and not only their money but, like Hugh, their time their services and their lives. Hugh didn't just ask for help, he offered his whole life and set the example himself. Jesus didn't just preach to others, He gave His own life also.

Being a Christian doesn't just mean occasional attendance at church, saying your prayers when you remember, and putting a coin in the offertory plate. Jesus doesn't want a part of us, He wants our whole lives; this is what it means when we call Jesus 'Lord.' It isn't how much you can afford, but giving your all that counts with God, taking Him into every part and corner of our lives and doing His will.

Prayer: O God, we thank you for life and health and vigour; for food and friends; for work and play and for all that makes life a joy; but most of all for the life Jesus gave for us all. Help us to give our lives for others as He did. *Amen.*

21. Sadhu Sundar Singh

A PARABLE OF MAN'S LOVE

Scripture Reading: Matthew 16:24–27.
Key Verse: 25. Whosoever will save his life shall lose it; whosoever will lose his life for My sake shall find it.
Hymn: O happy band of pilgrims.

The road from Nepal into Tibet is a dangerous one. The higher you go the narrower it gets until it finally is no more than a goat track, with the mountain soaring up high on one side, far too steep to climb, and dropping almost vertically down for thousands of feet on the other side. Because the land is so high ice lies permanently on the summits of some of the peaks, and snowstorms are not uncommon even in the summer. Yet because it is the most direct road some people use it despite the hazards.

One summer day, when the snow was driving horizontally, two men were taking this pass. One was a man who traded with the Nepalese and was on his way home. He had done this journey many times and so was properly dressed for such with a sheepskin coat over his pullovers and had thick boots and socks. The other, because he was a poor missionary, had only a thin cotton robe, saffron in colour to show that he was a 'holy man', and no shoes. He was Indian by birth and his name was Sundar Singh.

Sundar told the trader about Jesus who went about doing good and not caring for his own life, but the Tibetan replied that it was every man for himself in this world.

Presently the path was blocked by a mound almost covered with snow. The trader squeezed past but Sundar stopped, scraped away the snow and discovered that it was a man who had been overcome by the cold. Sundar called to the trader for help.

'It's too late to help him,' he replied, 'He'll die anyway, and so will we if we attempt to help him. He'll have to be carried and that will slow us up and we shan't reach the village before nightfall. I'm not going to risk my life in the dark. If you'll take my advice you'll forget your Christian ways and leave him and save yourself. That's what I'm going to do.' And he moved on.

Sundar had difficulty in getting the man on to his back, and the weight slowed him down, but after a while Sundar felt much warmer. The extra exertion of carrying the man had improved his circulation and generated more heat. So Sundar was able to press on a little faster. The warmth of Sundar's body crept through to the burden on his back and the man revived. After a few miles he was able to walk holding on to Sundar's arm.

Hours later, just as they came into sight of Ranget village, they found another man lying flat, almost covered with snow. It was the Tibetan trader who had refused to help to save another man. Now he was frozen to death. In trying to save his own life he had lost it. Sundar in being willing to lose his life for God and the man's sake, had saved it. This is what Jesus said in our reading.

This story illustrates the two kinds of people that there are in life, the selfish who are only concerned with their own welfare, like the trader, and the unselfish like Sundar Singh who spend the whole of their lives in the loving service of others. Which kind are you? Do you think about yourself first, or even exclusively, or do you put other people's needs before your own?

The proof of whether we truly love God and our fellow men will be seen in our actions towards others. Jesus said that we can't love Him unless we love our neighbours; that the amount that we cared for others was the amount we loved Him.

This story also illustrates the rewards of our living. God has promised real life, eternal life with Him to those who, for love of their fellow men are prepared to give up their lives here on this earth to serve them. The person who lacks love for men and uses the whole of his life for selfish ends will not have the heavenly reward. This is why Jesus went on, 'What shall it profit a man if he gain the whole world and lose his own soul?' Be wise, spend your life in the loving service of God and man now, and then enjoy God forever. With the help of Christ we can.

Prayer: O God, you have created us for your glory and service, so make us ready to help the weak with sympathetic hearts and willing hands. Where our love for our fellows is cold, warm it, where we lack it supply it, so that we may not falter in our love but continue faithful to the end. *Amen.*

22. *Astronaut Walks in Space*

A PARABLE OF ADVENTURING

Scripture Reading: John 14:1–3.
Key Verse: 3. Where I am ye may be also.
Hymn: Soldiers of Christ arise and put your armour on.

What would your answer be if I asked you what had been your greatest adventure? Perhaps the day you were lost when still a small child, or the first time you went off with only your friends and no parents for a picnic. If you are older perhaps you would remember your first attempt at mountain-climbing, even if the mountain was only a small one, and the excitement of wondering if you would fall or not. It may be your greatest adventure was flying in an aeroplane for the first time and realizing what a long way down it was if anything went wrong with the aero-engine. Perhaps you wished that you could keep contact with the earth at the same time as flying.

In all these things you will see that there is a wish to go off on your own, and yet a desire to keep in touch with those you love and who love you, just in case something goes wrong with your little adventure. This is why the radio on a boat or aeroplane is so important; in an emergency you can get in touch with those who can help.

Would you like to be an astronaut? They must be fond of adventure. At times when they fly round the back of the moon their radio communication with earth is cut off. Can you imagine how they feel when they find that they are in touch with earth again?

Do you recall the time when the first astronaut went for a walk in space? Did he just decide to step outside to get a bit of exercise and go off on his own, or did he make sure that he kept in close touch with his space-craft? Can you picture yourself out there? You will remember, I am sure, that he had a long, strong line attached to him. But did you know it had three purposes? The first you will know; it was so that he could be brought back to the ship. What were the other two? One was a pipe-line which supplied oxygen to enable the astronaut to breathe whilst outside the craft, a vital source of life. The other was the telephone-line so that he could talk to the captain inside the capsule and hence back to headquarters. Even with all three in one umbilical cord it must have been a thrilling adventure.

God knew all these three things before he made man. He has sent his own Son Jesus Christ for all three things for our safety.

Christ is our life-line. Just before He returned to heaven He said that He would send His Holy Spirit to take His place, and He did. The Holy Spirit is the breath of God that gives us life and power to conquer the trials and temptations in the walk of life. When the Holy Spirit fell on the disciples at the first Whitsun, these fearful men who fled when Jesus was arrested, suddenly became brave and faced the world and suffered punishment and exile or death rather than deny their faith in Jesus as God's Son.

Christ is our means of communication with headquarters. The Bible reminds us that there is only one mediator between God and man, and He is Jesus Christ. Jesus said that He was the only way to the Father. Whilst we have faith in Jesus Christ we can pray to Him and He will present our petitions to our heavenly Father. This line of communication is never cut off.

Christ is, most of all, our means of return to the Father. When we do wrong it is like cutting ourselves off from God. But God has sent Jesus to forgive our sins if we trust Him and to make a way back to heaven for us.

So Jesus is our source of eternal life, our means of communication with God, and our way back to God.

Jesus said, 'I go to prepare a place for you, that where I am there you may be also.' If we feel out alone in space, cut off from real life and safety, we have only to trust the threefold line of Jesus Christ and we shall be hauled back to the safety of God in his heaven.

Let us use one of these lines, the line of communication now.

Prayer: O God, our heavenly Father, we come to you in the Name of your Son Jesus Christ, to ask that in the great adventure of life we may never forget your presence with us. May your Holy Spirit guide us in our journey and give us strength to overcome all our problems, and may our faith in Jesus bring us at last safely home to you. *Amen.*

23. A Waste of Corn

A PARABLE OF HARVESTING

Scripture Reading: John 12:23–33.
Key Verse: 24. Except a corn of wheat fall into the ground and die, it abideth alone; but if it die it bringeth forth much fruit.
Hymn: We plough the fields and scatter.

Thank you for all the gifts you have brought for the poorer people who live near us. This morning as I came in I overheard one boy say, 'What a waste.' I suppose he meant that it was a waste giving it to old people who usually don't have large appetites, when he could have done it more justice with his large capacity for food. Yesterday at school dinners we didn't think it a waste to give him two helpings of the first course, and three helpings of the sweet that followed. Is it a waste to give all this harvest away?

A mole, who is noted for his huge appetite and readiness to eat any form of meat he can find underground at any time of the day, once tunnelled through a newly planted cornfield. Everywhere he went there were seeds of corn.

'Pity I don't like cereals,' he said, 'but fancy the farmer throwing away so much good seed. It's a terrible waste,' and he moved to another field.

Several months later he returned to this field, but the corn seeds were nowhere to be seen. In fact the mole found it difficult to penetrate far into the field, for whichever way he went there was a fence of cornstalks, like a thick forest of sticks. So he turned and went out thinking, 'I knew it was a waste of grain. There wasn't a single seed left in that field so far as I could see.' But that was the trouble; down below ground he couldn't see. If he had come up to the surface he would have seen what had happened. Each single seed had sprouted and had produced a stalk with an ear full of corn seeds. It was no waste, it was a grand harvest. The farmer knew when he sowed the corn that he wasn't wasting it. He knew that he had to sacrifice it if it were to multiply.

This is what Jesus meant when He said, 'Except a seed of wheat fall into the ground and die, it abideth alone; but if it die it bringeth forth much fruit.' The disciples understood that Jesus was referring to Himself; that He would soon be dead and buried like a seed of wheat, but they didn't listen to the rest and thought like the mole what a waste of a good, young life that would be. But we know now that Jesus had to die to pay the price of our sins so that we might go to make God's harvest of souls in heaven. The corn seed of Jesus' life by being buried, brought forth much fruit. Think of the size of the Christian Church all over the world, past as well as present; what a harvest that is going to be! Did Jesus waste His life when He permitted His body to be buried?

What He did with His life, He wants us to do with our own, to be willing to spend our lives for the benefits of others. Today we have done this in making a sacrifice to buy food for needy people. Last year the prefects distributed large parcels of all kinds of harvest food, and when they came back you could see how happy it had made them. They spoke of the thanks they had received from the old folk, and how one poor lady had said, 'Thank God,' for that morning she had prayed to God for someone to bring her some food as her larder was empty.

Many people today or tomorrow will thank God for your gifts. Whilst God has produced the foods, you have brought them and sacrificed in order to feed poor and needy folk. You have been used by God, and God is grateful as well as the old people living around us.

Has this Harvest Festival been a waste? Those who get the parcels don't think so. God doesn't think so. I hope you don't. Let us thank God that he has given so much to us that we have enough and to spare.

Prayer: O God, our heavenly Father, we praise you that once more you have kept your promise that while the earth remains there will always be both seedtime and harvest. We thank you for all the food you have so generously provided for us. We ask you now to bless the gifts we have gladly brought for others that they may bring joy as well as relief to those in need. *Amen.*

24. *To Live or not to Live*

A PARABLE OF EASTER

Scripture Reading: 1 Corinthians 15:9–23.
Key Verse: 22. *As in Adam all die, even so in Christ shall all be made alive.*
Hymn: Christ the Lord is risen today.

Some boys were discussing the most important thing in life. Food, sport, fun, fame, power, and money were suggested and discarded in turn. At last one said, 'Staying alive.' That was nearer to the truth wasn't it? But not all the truth. Life itself is wonderful, isn't it? Think of trees, flowers, birds, fishes, animals, especially young ones, and babies.

Freddy Tait came to learn about the wonder of life through potatoes. He was too young to go to school, so he played in the house in the winter, but when spring came he went into the large, lovely garden.

One day he saw Adam, the gardener working in the kitchen-garden, and went to watch. Adam had a large sack of potatoes and was dropping them one by one into trenches which he had prepared. Then he turned the soil over, covering the potatoes and trod the earth down firmly all round them.

'Why d'you bury all those lovely potatoes?' asked Freddy.

'You watch the ground for a few weeks and you'll see,' said Adam. So Freddy watched. He saw what he thought were weeds growing all over the ground, and then they began to die off. One day the gardener called Freddy who came running.

'Watch and you'll see why I buried the potatoes,' said Adam, and he took a large fork and dug up each plant. To Freddy's amazement, instead of there being one dead potato in each spot there were many, and as Adam went down each row hundreds were revealed. The dead potatoes had come to life and multiplied.

When the ground had been cleared, Freddy asked if he could use the empty plot and then hurried indoors. He came out with a couple of boxes, as much as he could hold. He opened one and took out some small, white, round balls. Then he put them in holes all over the ground and covered them up and trod on them just as he had seen Adam do. Adam said nothing. Freddy Tait's father was a famous golfer, and Freddy thought to do his father a good turn by multiplying his golf-balls for him. He waited weeks but no plants grew and at last he took a little trowel and began to dig. The gardener just watched.

When Freddy had retrieved all the balls that he had planted he said, 'These balls don't work.' Adam then explained that there were live things and dead things. The live things could produce other live things like themselves, as the potatoes had done. But dead things couldn't produce themselves. The difference was that the living things were made by God, and the dead things by man.

No man has ever produced a living thing from dead materials. Life is wonderful because it comes from God. The Bible says that God made man; and what He has made He can make again. So is life the most important thing in the world? When Freddy Tait grew up he sacrificed his life to save others. He had found something more important than life; love for others.

Jesus gave His life too, because He loved us. But Easter reminds us that He came back to life, rose from the grave, and promised, 'Because I live, you shall live also.'

Because Adam sinned in the Garden of Eden, death comes to everyone. But because Jesus rose from the dead, so shall we. 'As in Adam all die, even so in Jesus Christ shall all be made alive.'

Where we spend that resurrection life largely depends upon what we think is the most important thing in life. Is it just staying alive, or living it well, or being prepared to lay it down for the love of God and our fellow-men?

Prayer: Eternal Father, we praise you that in this springtime you remind us in bud, and leaf, and flower that that which was dead can come to newness of life. We thank you that in Jesus Christ your Son you have overcome temptation, sin and death, and opened for us the way to everlasting life. We ask you that by your Holy Spirit we may believe the truth of life after death and enjoy it with you eternally. *Amen.*

25. *God's Messengers*

A PARABLE OF CONSCIENCE

Scripture Reading: Genesis 3.
Key Verse: 1 Timothy 1:19. . . . hold on to your faith and a good conscience . . . which some have put away and been wrecked.
Hymn: Awake my soul, and with the sun.

With radio covering the whole world, and weather ships stationed in many parts of every ocean, and sea-going vessels being large crafts, the danger of shipwreck from storm is small today. But hundreds of years ago sailors had frail boats and had to keep their own eyes open for signs of bad weather. Risking their lives daily in this way, they became superstitious and were careful not to do anything which they thought was unlucky. More wisely, they also prayed that they would be protected. Many prayed to the mother of Jesus, and called her, 'Mother Dear'. In those days the language of the church was latin, so the sailors used the words, 'Mater Cara'. Later it became corrupted to 'Mother Carey.'

Storm petrels which only come to land to nest, were thought to be unlucky birds because they were usually seen just before a storm, when the wind would whip up the waves making it easy for the petrels to catch the small fish which were thrown up. It was for this reason the petrels flew low or hovered over the sea, making it look as though they were walking on the sea. This is how they got their name, for Peter walked on the water to Jesus, and 'petrello' means 'little Peter'.

When the sailors prayed to 'Mother Carey' for protection from storms at sea, and thse petrels began to 'walk on the water' just before a storm, they believed them to be messengers from her to warn them of approaching danger. So they called them 'Mother Carey's chickens', a name which persists among mariners to this day. Those who disregarded this warning found out to their cost how foolish they had been.

Ever since God made man, God has been sending messages to him, often warning him to beware of danger. In the Garden of Eden God warned Adam that if he ate from one particular tree he would suffer. But Adam disobeyed God, ate of the forbidden fruit and was cast out of the garden. In this way he obtained from personal experience, a knowledge of good and evil, good being obedience to the known will of God, and evil being disobedience to His will. He disobeyed God and found that it didn't pay. In this way his conscience was awakened. So is ours too. Each time we do something good we are happy in our minds. When we do something that we know is wrong, that is against God's will, then we have a guilty conscience and feel miserable. If we are wise we listen to our conscience, God's messenger, and the voice becomes clearer, and as we obey it more and more our lives become happier and more peaceful. The more we disregard our conscience, the fainter God's warning voice becomes, and it is possible, in the end not to hear it at all.

Did you hear about the boy who was going to work for the first time? He had to be up early so he set his alarm-clock to give him plenty of time. When it went off in the morning, he remembered that he had given himself more than enough time and slept on for a while, and then had to rush to get to work on time. That night he decided to set the clock to give him just enough time so that he wouldn't be tempted to sleep on. When the alarm went off in the morning he only heard it as though in a dream, it only half woke him and he was a little late for work. The third morning the alarm went off but he slept through it. He got the sack. His mind had got used to hearing it and not obeying it, so that in the end the warning didn't register at all. It is the same with our conscience. When it speaks to us we should heed its warning at once. It is wise to trust God and obey His voice, for to ignore it is to be shipwrecked. This is what Paul meant when he said to Timothy. 'Hold on to your faith and keep a good conscience, which some have ignored and their lives been wrecked.' We will be wise to be quick to respond to our conscience.

Prayer: Sharpen our ears, O Lord, to listen to the voice of conscience, so that we may learn to distinguish good from evil. Give us love for the good, and a ready will to perform it, and a hatred for that which is base and evil so that we may overcome it. So teach us your way and strengthen us to walk in it. *Amen.*

26. *The Best Policy*

A PARABLE OF HONESTY

Scripture Reading: Joshua 6:18, 19; 7:1, 2, 5, 6, 10–14, 16–21, 25, 26.

Key Verse: 6:18. Keep yourselves from the accursed thing, lest you make yourselves accursed, when you take of the accursed thing, and make the camp of Israel a curse and trouble it.

Hymn: Fight the good fight.

The proverb, 'honesty is the best policy', is a wise one, but its wisdom is not always recognized. There will always be those who covet and steal hoping to 'get away with it'. Achan in our reading this morning, was one of these. The city of Jericho had fallen to the Israelites, God having made the walls to crumble. Joshua commanded that the Israelites did no looting for themselves. After this battle they were approaching the next town Ai, and sent out spies to estimate its strength. These thought that a small army would be enough to conquer it, and such was sent. But they were routed by the men of Ai and thirty-six were killed. This made Joshua ask God for the reason. God told him that someone had stolen from Jericho against orders, and until the thief confessed He would not help Israel. Dishonesty was sin and it had to be punished. God also told Joshua how to give the thief every chance to confess. Joshua made the tribes pass one at a time before him, and he picked out one tribe. Then he made that tribe split into separate families and had them pass one by one and he chose one family. He divided that family into households and picked out one, and then made each member of that group pass by individually. Joshua called out Achan and told him to confess because he was the one that was troubling his family and tribe and nation. Then Achan admitted stealing a fine robe, 200 shekels of silver and fifty shekels of gold, which he had hidden in the ground beneath his tent. The stolen articles were retrieved, Achan punished, and then God gave the Israelites victory over Ai at the next encounter.

When a child steals he brings dishonour and trouble upon himself, his family, his school, and as we have seen in Achan, upon his race. Compare this story with another one.

It happened in the days when white men had settled in North America and finished fighting the Red Indians, and tobacco-smoking was becoming popular and its dangers not yet known. A Red Indian working with some white men who were smoking, asked if he could try it. The foreman put his hand into his pocket where he kept his loose tobacco leaves, and gave the native a handful. The following day the Indian went to the man who had given him the tobacco and offered him a small coin. 'I don't want paying,' the white man said. The Indian replied, 'This your money not mine. I find it in smoke leaves.'

'Why didn't you keep it?' the foreman asked.

'Good man and bad man in here,' the honest Indian replied pointing to his heart, 'Bad man him say "Keep" good man say "Give back" so they talk all night, I get no sleep. Now I give back I feel good, get plenty sleep.'

It pays to be honest. The Red Indian couldn't sleep until he had done the honest thing. I don't suppose Achan could either, fearing someone would find him out. When we do this kind of wrong our conscience keeps troubling us and gives us no rest. If we are wise we put things right at once.

Perhaps you think that you are always honest. In the parable of the talents, Jesus praised those who had put their talents to good use, but condemned the one who had not used his for the benefit of someone else. Joshua and the Israelites were given special privileges by God, but He expected that they would not be abused. When they were, He was displeased and withdrew His favours. When they repented He restored His blessings. When we abuse or waste the gifts of life, health, strength and ability that God has given us we must not be surprised if He withdraws them.

We must be honest with God as well as with man. Well might Joshua say, 'Keep yourselves from stealing, lest you make your nation as well as your family and yourself troubled.'

Prayer: Heavenly Father, we want to be straight and honest in all that we do, whether it is towards you or mankind. Prevent us by your Holy Spirit, from praising good deeds whilst practising evil ones, and grant that what we say with our lips we may honestly practise in our lives. This we ask in the Name of Jesus Christ our Lord. *Amen.*

27. *God's Commands*

A PARABLE OF THE BEGINNING OF TERM

Scripture Reading: Isaiah 55:1–7.
Key Verses: 3. Come unto Me; hear and your soul shall live.
6. Seek the Lord.
Hymn: Through all the changing scenes of life.

We don't like people telling us what we must do. But very often it is wiser to obey commands. Consider the Road Safety signs for instance. If the sign at a cross-road says 'Halt' and you ride your bicycle straight on, you may not ride your cycle again. 'Stop, look, listen,' is another command before crossing a road, that may save our lives if we obey it. But God's commands are more important than man's. In today's reading there were three, 'come, hear, seek.'

Let us consider the command 'Come'! There was once a very rich man who lived in a large mansion. He had a butler, a housekeeper, a cook, many maids, a valet, a chaffeur, and many gardeners; in fact he had someone to do everything for him. In consequence he fell sick with indigestion and bad stomach pains. His doctor came and advised him to get some exercise, play tennis or swim or walk a mile every day around his grounds, and then his health would improve. But he had got so used to having things done for him that he arranged for the maids to play tennis for him, some garden boys to swim in his private pool, and the butler to walk the mile a day for him. His pains got no better and he cursed the doctor for a fool. Finally the butler pleaded, 'Sir, if you would only try a walk yourself.'

Foolish though wealthy, wasn't he? 'Come for a walk, come for a swim, come for a game of tennis,' but he didn't come. Aren't you just as foolish if when you are told that you must come to school, you don't, and think that as your brother goes there's no need for you to go. If you are to earn a good living you must first learn, and you can only do this if you yourself come to school. Your future depends upon coming to school. Come!

The second command is 'Listen.' A favourite party game when I was young was 'King of the ring.' Silence was essential. The king sat blindfolded in the centre of a ring of children seated cross-legged and with arms folded. The object was for a child to rise, walk to the king silently and pretend to stab him. If he did this he became king. If, however, the king heard the slightest noise and pointed in the direction of the would-be assassin, he saved his life and another would try. His 'life' depended upon his listening well. This is true in school too. Even if you do come to school you won't learn much if you don't listen to the teacher. Your future depends upon listening in school.

The third command is 'seek' or 'search'. When a child doesn't come home at an expected time, the parents get anxious and start to search. Later friends join in, and if this proves useless the police are told and perhaps hundreds of policemen comb the area until the missing child is found. Can you imagine your parents not searching for you if you were lost? In school you are asked to search. Problems are put and you have to seek the answer. It may mean perusing many books in the library, or doing various experiments in the laboratory. If you persist in the search you will find what you are looking for. You may come to school, and you may listen, but if you don't search for knowledge you may fail to attain your object· Your future depends upon it.

All this also applies to Morning Worship. In the verses that we read, Isaiah was prophesying that the Kingdom of God will be much better than on earth, but it will only be attained by seeking for God, coming to God, and listening to His commands and obeying them. Do you come to assembly or try to dodge it? Do you really listen for God's voice in every part of our worship? Are you determined to search diligently for God until you find Him? If you come and listen and search for God and for knowledge each day this term you will find them both. Your future, here and hereafter, depends upon your obedience to these commands of God. Come! Hear! Seek!

Prayer: Loving Father, we thank you for the joy of the holidays and the opportunity of another new term. Help us to come regularly, to listen attentively and to search diligently, for knowledge and a consciousness of your presence, and grant that all that we do, from Morning Worship to home bell, everyday, may please thee. *Amen.*

28. *I'm Last*

A PARABLE OF GOOD FRIDAY

Scripture Reading: Mark 15:15–28.
Key Verse: John 15:13. Greater love hath no man than this that a man lay down his life for his friends.
Hymn: There is a green hill.

Rosaline had pinned a note on the outside of her bedroom door. It read, 'I am last.' Her uncle, a schoolteacher, was disappointed when he read it. He mentioned it to her at meal-time. 'You didn't do so well in your school examinations, I see,' he said. Rosaline didn't answer at once, but her mother was quick to say. 'Not well! I'd like to know how much better she could have done. She came top!' Rosaline saw that her uncle didn't understand, so she explained, 'The note on my door doesn't refer to examinations uncle; last Good Friday at chapel, I realized for the first time that Jesus had died on the Cross for me, and how unselfish this was. This note is to remind me that Jesus must be first, others second, and myself last. I think that's more important than coming top, even though I know Jesus wants me to do my best in school.' Where do you put yourself? Do you say, 'I'm aboard Jack, pull up the ladder'? We all know what that means, 'Self first, self second, anything left self again.' Would you give your life to help others, or is your main concern to help yourself?

In the sixteenth century Portuguese traders sailed past a long island off the coast of China. It was so lovely with its lilies and orchids in bloom and the deep green of the citrus trees, that they called it 'Ilha Formosa,' or 'Beautiful Island' and the name stuck. But the natural beauty of the island of Formosa was a direct contrast to the ugly nature of its people. They were cannibals and head-hunters especially in the more mountainous parts. The savage custom of human sacrifice was allowed to continue until a young Chinese governor named Gohu was appointed. He hated this senseless waste of life. By gentle example and extreme efforts to improve the standard of living he gradually won very many round to his more humane way of life. Things went well until a long spell of dry weather began to wither the crops. The ground hardened, the streams dried up until animals began to die, and the lives of the people were threatened. Their pagan religious leaders began to clamour for the people to return to their old way of life, and promised rain as soon as the anger of their gods had been placated with a human sacrifice once more. Gohu did his best to dissuade them but when he saw that they would take someone no matter what he said, then he agreed. 'All right,' he said, 'but you must let me choose the victim. Gather at your sacred grove just before dawn and a man clothed from head to foot in a red robe with a hood will appear. Kill him quickly and offer him to your gods.' As the sun rose the next morning the hooded man came into view. A priest struck with his long knife and the man fell dead at his feet. A cry of dismay and regret escaped from his lips when he uncovered the man's face. It was Gohu who had sacrificed himself to save another. No human sacrifice has since been offered on Formosa. Gohu put himself last, least of all.

On Good Friday we remember another who offered Himself as a sacrifice. He had committed no sin, had gone about doing good and healing the sick and raising the dead. He had preached, 'Greater love hath no man than this that a man lay down his life for his friend.' He also practised it; and He did it not only for His friends but for His enemies too. He was able to overcome because of His great love for God and for men. The notice over the Cross might well have read, 'I'm last.' As we give thanks for Jesus who died in our place, let us determine also to say, 'God first, others second, self last.'

Prayer: Almighty God, who because of your great love have sent your Son Jesus Christ to suffer death upon the Cross for us, help us to follow the example of His love for you and for all men from this day forward and until you call us to be with you for ever. *Amen.*

29. *What is a Friend?*

A PARABLE OF FRIENDSHIP

Scripture Reading: John 15:10–17.
Key Verse: 14. You are My friends if you do what I command you.
Hymn: O Jesus I have promised.

How many friends have you? Two or three, or a lot? If you had to write down their names you would first put those who are your best friends, those you have no doubts about, and later you would think of others that you were not sure about, and you would have to ask yourself, 'What is a friend?'

The other day I stopped two boys fighting. When I questioned one about it he said, 'But sir, he's my friend.' A slight difference of opinion came between these two boys who called themselves friends, and they fought over it. Were they friends? How do you decide who is a friend? What makes a friend?

When the missionary Mildred Cable was travelling through the Gobi Desert her company decided to make camp as evening was beginning to fall. They lit a fire and sat around while they waited for the meal to cook. Presently a soldier from a frontier garrison scores of miles away staggered into the circle almost exhausted. He was given some refreshment and was invited to stay, but he explained why he could not remain. He had not come for himself but for a friend who was ill and resting in a cave not too far away, and he had hoped that they would have some medicine for his comrade. When asked why he was so exhausted if his camp was near by, he told them that he had no camp, that he and his friend had been travelling many days without food or shelter. It seemed that he was a deserter and when directly asked this he removed the scarf that had been tied over his head and showed that one ear had been cut off. Mildred knew then that this soldier had deserted before and had been caught and suffered the penalty for desertion. She also knew that if he were caught now, after running away a second time, he would be flogged to death. The sick friend was brought to the missionary camp and tended.

'Why do you risk your life waiting to help this man when you need to get away as quickly as possible if you are not to be caught?' Mildred asked. The soldier hesitated and then said, 'We deserted together. When he took sick I couldn't leave him to die alone in the desert even if it cost me my life. He's my friend.' Eventually both reached safety and reported the extreme punishments and terrible conditions in the garrison.

We can see that this man was a true friend. He was willing to give his life for the other. Jesus said, 'Greater love hath no man than this that a man lay down his life for his friend.'

The sufferer had begged, 'Get some help or I'll die.' His friend did all that was asked of him. 'You are My friends,' said Jesus, 'if you do as I command you.'

The soldier could have left the sick one to die and gone on alone to save his own life, but he wouldn't forsake him in his need. Jesus said to His disciples, 'I have called you friends.' But when He was arrested they all forsook Him and fled. Jesus was their friend, but were they His friends?

Judas Iscariot, one of the disciples, betrayed Jesus for money and led the Temple guards to where Jesus was. To show them in the darkness who Jesus was, he went up to Jesus and kissed Him. '*Friend,*' said Jesus, 'betrayest thou the Son of Man with a kiss?' Judas wasn't Jesus' friend for he betrayed Him. Jesus was Judas' friend in spite of this, and His later crucifixion.

What makes a friend? The soldier in our story was a true friend because he shared the others troubles, because he did what the sick one asked, and because he risked a flogging and death for him and didn't betray him. Jesus is a true friend of ours because He shares our troubles, answers our prayer requests, doesn't betray us and has suffered flogging and death for us. But are we His friends, do we keep His commandments, do we let Him down? We don't deserve His friendship, but in spite of our weaknesses He remains our friend. Do you know what makes a friend now? Let us try to be worthy of His friendship.

Prayer: Lord Jesus, we thank you for being a friend to us and for giving your life to save us from the penalty for our wrong-doing. Help us, by your Holy Spirit, never to make use of our friends for our own benefit, but always to put our friends' needs before our own. Help us always to behave loyally to them and to you, so that we may find full satisfaction in all our friendships. *Amen.*

30. What's that in your Hand?

A PARABLE OF SERVICE

Scripture Reading: Exodus 3:1–14; 4:1–5.
Key Verse: 4:2. What is that in your hand?
Hymn: Teach me My God and King.

Just before his sixteenth birthday Deauville Walker made it pretty obvious to his parents that he would like a camera for his birthday present. The day came and sure enough there was the camera. Deauville looked surprised and was quick to thank his mother and father. They warned him to be careful as it was loaded with a film.

Now it happened to be Sunday and they always went to church. Deauville couldn't bear to be parted from his new camera and asked if he might take it with him. His parents said that he could if he would promise not to play with it in church.

The Bible reading that morning was the passage we read earlier. The minister in his sermon told the story of how God called Moses to be the leader of the children of Israel out of bondage in Egypt to a new land that they should have for themselves; that Moses protested that he was not the right man for such a job; that he wasn't trained as a leader, that he wasn't a good public speaker and that the people wouldn't listen to him because he hadn't any authority over the Israelites. Then the minister called out just as God had to Moses, 'What's that in your hand?' Deauville had been dreaming about what he would do with his new camera and was awakened by the minister's shout and quickly replied, 'A camera.' The minister smiled and went on telling how Moses' rod which he had in his hand was used by God to do very wonderful things to assure Moses that the people would accept him. When the service ended and the congregation filed out, the minister was at the door and as Deauville shook his hand he said 'Make sure that you use that which you have in your hand to serve God as Moses used his rod for God.'

Deauville wanted to serve God and planned to be a missionary. He studied hard and passed his examinations and actually got to the mission-field, but he found that he wasn't very good at talking to the natives and even thought of returning home. But he had been using his camera to take photographs of the country and the people and some of these were sent home by the missionary in charge of the station and were printed in the missionary magazines. As a result of these pictures many people were spurred into sending gifts of clothing and money. And so Deauville was kept there for just this purpose, and he used what was in his hand, a camera for God's service.

If you had gone to visit Florence Nightingale when she was a little girl you would always have found her with a bandage in her hand, and you would have seen her dolls all bandaged and her dog with a splint on his tail. If she had heard the minister cry, 'What's that in your hand?' she would have replied, 'A bandage.' When she grew to be a woman the Crimean War was being fought and after a while it became known that 30,000 men were sick or wounded and there was no one to care for them. Florence was quick to offer her services, but they were refused because for one reason the battle-front was no place for a woman, and secondly that it would cost £30,000 to equip such a force and that was more than the country could afford at that time. Florence rounded up a body of women who were anxious to help and invited her friends to subscribe the needed money, which they promptly did. Florence went and the soldiers were full of praises for 'The Lady of the Lamp', as she became known. Countless lives were saved and also as a result of this, when she returned home a nursing service came into being for the first time. She had a bandage in her hand and she used it for God.

Jesus used His hands for God. He not only laid them on the sick and healed them, but He stretched His hands out on the Cross to pay the penalty for our misdeeds and bring us into His Kingdom.

Find out what you have in your hand, what you are best at, and offer it to God and you will find that God will bless it and use it for His glory.

Prayer: O God, you have created us and given us all different talents for your glory and service. Help us by your Holy Spirit to develop to the uttermost those gifts which can best be used by you, and then give us the grace to spend and be spent in the service of others. For the sake of Jesus Christ our Lord. *Amen.*

31. The Odd Twins

A PARABLE OF WHITSUNTIDE

Scripture Reading: Acts 2:1–8, 12–24, 32, 33.
Key Verse: 8. You shall receive power after that the Holy Spirit has come upon you.
Hymn: Our blest Redeemer.

Christopher and Gary were twins and they were alike as two peas, yet you could always tell them apart because Chris always had a pleasant face whilst Gary was always sullen. This was because of their differing natures. Chris was well-mannered, patient and industrious, and in consequence, did well at school and received the success and praise that he deserved. Yet he remained humble and was always ready to run an errand or help anyone in need. Gary, though just as intelligent as his brother was lazy, so didn't do so well. He attempted to excuse himself by saying, 'I didn't try. I could have done as well as Chris if I had wanted to.' He was often rude to those who tried to show him how foolish he was, and if they persisted, he would get in a temper. So the two became less and less alike in character, and it showed in their faces.

Chris would occasionally talk to Gary about asking God to help him, for Chris was very concerned about Gary's behaviour, and he prayed daily for him. Sometimes Gary would hit out at Chris in his jealousy, but Chris was always ready to forgive and forget because he loved his wayward brother. Gary wished he was like his brother but was too proud to change.

The neighbours often commented on the difference in the boys, 'Chris is such a nice lad. He'll go a long way. But Gary will come to a sticky end, you mark my words.' Chris went up to the University and it looked as though the prophecies concerning him would prove to be true. But Chris fell sick and died quite suddenly. Everyone was shocked and sad and some even wished that it had happened to his brother instead. Gary felt it most of all and the improvement in his conduct was attributed to the death of Chris. His temper got better, he spoke more politely, settled down to serious work and found time to help the needy also. 'What a change in him,' the neighbours said. 'He might even take Christopher's place and achieve something useful. It's a pity that Chris had to die to make it happen though.' This time their prophecies were correct. Gary became first a councillor and later a Member of Parliament, and was much sought after as lay-preacher. Sometimes he would tell his congregations the cause of the change in his way of life.

'It wasn't till Chris died that I fully realized how stupid I had been. I asked God to help me, and from then on I didn't want to do the wrong things anymore. The good advice that Chris had given me came readily to my mind, and soon I began to think and act like him. It was as though Chris' mind came into mine and has stayed there ever since. I feel as though Chris is living in me.'

Something like this happened the first Whitsun. Just before His ascension, Jesus appeared to His disciples and told them that the Holy Spirit which had dwelt in Him would be given to them, and they would be able to do the wonderful things that He had done. And that is exactly what happened. Forty days later, a hundred and twenty followers of Jesus were in a room together when suddenly the Holy Spirit of Jesus came upon them and they were all changed in their spirits. Peter was perhaps the most changed. Nicknamed Boanerges, a Son of Thunder, because of his quick temper, he learned to control it. Big as he was, he was a coward having denied that he knew Jesus. After his baptism in the Holy Spirit he feared no one and told the priests and the people in Jerusalem that in crucifying Jesus they had killed God's own Son. The day following he healed a lame man and he continued to do the things Jesus only had done before until his own crucifixion. Like Gary he might have said, 'It was as though His spirit released from His body entered mine.' This is exactly what did happen to Peter. And it can happen to us. Paul says, 'Let this mind be in you which was also in Christ Jesus . . . If any man have not the spirit of Christ he is none of His,' and Jesus promised, 'You shall receive power after that the Holy Spirit is come upon you.'

Prayer: O God we praise you that at this time of the year you sent your Holy Spirit into the hearts and lives of those that loved you. Fill us we pray with that same Holy Spirit that the mind of Jesus may be in us to guide and control all our thoughts and actions evermore, to your praise and glory. *Amen.*

32. Give Me a Light

A PARABLE OF LIGHT

Scripture Reading: Matthew 5:14–16.

Key Verses: 16. Let your light so shine before men that they may see your good works and glorify your Father in heaven.

John 8:12. I am the Light of the World . . . he that followeth Me shall have the light of life.

Hymn: Immortal, invisible, God only wise.

Jesus said that He was the Light of the World. He also told His followers that they were the light of the world. This is simply explained. When you have a birthday cake and you are asked to light the candles you do not keep using matches. You light one candle with a match and then light all the others with it. The light of one candle can make all the others to shine. Jesus is the Light of the World, and we can be the same by getting our light from him.

A long time ago, before electric or gas or oil lighting, people had to use candles. Franz and Albrecht were two Swiss boys. Franz had a rich father and lived in a big house with a lot of ground. Albrecht's father worked on the estate and had a log house near by. Franz and Albrecht walked to school in the town together each day, and each carried a candle to see to work by in class. Other boys remarked that they were like their candles, for big, robust Franz had a large, fat candle, whilst lean Albrecht had a short, thin candle.

One day Franz took offence at something that Albrecht said, and though Albrecht apoligized and said that Franz had misunderstood him, the big lad strode off saying that he would go his own way to school, taking the short cut. Albrecht tried to warn Franz that as it was winter with the snow piled high, the short cut which they took in the spring and summer would be impossible. Franz completely ignored him.

When Albrecht arrived at school and lit his candle from the master's, it was clear to see that Franz had not arrived for his desk was in darkness. Albrecht didn't wait long. He blew his candle out and explained to the master that he was going to find Franz. When he reached the place where they had parted he followed the footprints of Franz in the snow. It was an hour before Albrecht found him. The depth of snow had been too much for him and he had been too proud to turn back. He was lying unconscious almost covered by drifting snow. Another half-hour and he would not have been found. Weak though he felt, Albrecht dragged Franz to a tree and propped him up, paused for a moment to ask God for strength, and then with a tremendous effort, lifted Franz on to his back like carrying a large bundle of firewood which was one of his daily chores. The journey home took a long while, and Albrecht had to rest several times, but at last they arrived. Franz was unconscious for two days.

As soon as he recovered he asked who had brought him back and upon being told he sent for Albrecht, apologized, and asked him, 'How did a little chap like you manage to carry a big fellow like me so far, and in deep snow?'

Albrecht replied, 'I asked God to help and strengthen me. He did.' Franz promised never to quarrel again and asked to know more about Albrecht's God. His candle was smaller but he shed more light than those of his fellows because he trusted in God.

He became a doctor with a large practice and began to get rich. Years later an epidemic overran Northern Italy and Albrecht left everything to minister to the poor and needy and dying. He saved many lives, but eventually through overwork and lack of proper nourishment, his resistances weakened and he caught the complaint and died. From that darkness he entered into the glorious light of the Presence of Jesus.

Jesus was his light of life, and Albrecht got his light, his courage and bravery and love of others from Him, and in turn became a light of helpfulness and love himself. If we follow Jesus, we shall have the light of His life; then we will let our light shine to others in our good works, and seeing them they will thank God.

Prayer: Lord Jesus Christ, we thank you for being the Light of the World. Help us to catch the flame of your Spirit that your life may shine through our actions and enlighten the lives of others, and so extend your Kingdom and glorify your Name. *Amen.*

33. *It's Catching*

A PARABLE OF INFLUENCE

Scripture Reading: John 1:35–50.
Key Verse: Romans 14:7. None of us lives to himself.
Hymn: The wise may bring their learning.

Coughs and sneezes spread diseases! We've all seen it on posters in school. We are encouraged to use a handkerchief to prevent the spread of germs because they are catching. Influenza is even worse; it can cause a serious epidemic. At the end of 1969, nearly three thousand people died each week from this complaint. They all caught it from someone else.

The word 'influenza' comes from an Italian word which means, 'a flowing out from one life to another.' It doesn't tell us anything about the sickness itself, only that it is catching. Nobody likes being confined to bed for many days, much less the feeling of extreme cold whilst the body is burning hot, and the taking of unpleasant tablets, to say nothing of the use of endless handkerchiefs, and the ache in head, body and legs. No, it's not good and it's catching. Our word 'influence' comes from this word, because it flows out of one person into another; influence however, can be good as well as bad.

Johnny Travers was eleven. He was leaving the Primary School with a bad attendance record. His parents were fined for his truancy more than once. When the magistrate heard that Johnny would be going to the Secondary School the next term he said that he hoped it would help Johnny not to truant again.

And so it seemed. All the first term Johnny was regular. So many new things to do, visits out of school, weekly trips to the public swimming-baths, experiments in the laboratory to do himself and the excitement of the handicraft shops and the art studios, all kept him busy and happy. Then one day in the second term he forgot to do some homework and instead of coming to school and explaining to the teacher, he decided not to go to school. This continued for several days and Johnny was fed up with no one to play with, so, one evening he spoke to one of his classmates named Tom, and told him how much better it was in the park than in school, and how he had truanted many times and hadn't had to suffer for it. So the next day Johnny had a friend with whom to help pass the time. After a week of walking round the park they got bored with this and played in some condemned houses. One day they found a locked cupboard and Johnny broke it open and they took away scores of little toys in boxes which they found there. As the toys were all the same they gave many away and sold others. The police noticing so many of these toys about began to inquire and so traced the toys back to Johnny' This offence, 'stealing by finding' brought Johnny and Tommy into Court. The magistrate was disappointed that Johnny hadn't settled in his new school and sent him to an approved school. Tom was put on probation and warned that he would follow Johnny if he didn't make good. But Tom had got a taste for adventure and continued to be troublesome. His headmaster was concerned for him and discovered that Tom had been friendly with a good lad named David before going astray with Johnny. So he asked David to win Tom's friendship back. This he did. David invited Tom home to tea, and later introduced him to other boys at his church club, and soon Tom found himself following David in all the good things that he did just as he had followed Johnny in all his bad deeds. Influence is catching, both good and bad.

Many children are easily led. If they are influenced by a bad companion then it leads them into trouble. But if they are influenced by good friends it leads to happiness.

The disciples were wise. Andrew was influenced by John the Baptist to follow Jesus. Andrew influenced his brother Peter to do the same and Philip influenced Nathanael to follow Jesus and their lives were happy and they influenced many others. They were wise; they followed Jesus, One who was a great influence for good. If we are wise we will follow Him too. When Paul said, 'None of us lives to himself,' he meant that everyone influences others for good or evil. Which sort of influence are you? If we let Christ influence us we shall influence others for good.

Prayer: Thank you God for all who are a good influence in this school. Help us to put Jesus first in our thoughts words and actions so that we may influence others for good. *Amen.*

34. Saint Christopher

A PARABLE OF LEAVERS

Scripture Reading: 1 Chronicles 29:1–12, 26–28.
Key Verse: 5. Who is willing to consecrate his service this day to the Lord?
Hymn: The Lord's my Shepherd.

Do you possess a St. Christopher medallion? Do you really think that it will protect you? Do you know the legend? Christopher was a very tall, strong warrior who lived in the fourth century after Christ. He felt that, as the mightiest of men he should only serve the greatest and best master, and he set out to find him. Men told him of one king who was greater than all the others, and so Christopher found him and offered him his services. The king made him his personal bodyguard. One day in court when the king was being entertained by a minstrel Christopher saw his master make the sign of the Cross with his finger whenever the Devil's name was mentioned in the song. When asked the reason why he did this, the king said that he was afraid that if he didn't the Devil would get power over him. 'If this is so,' Christopher said, 'then the Devil is greater than you and I am off to serve him.' And he went.

He travelled only a short distance, for the Devil, knowing Christopher's desire, made himself available to him. Seeing the Devil but not recognizing him, he asked him how he might find the Devil as he sought to serve him as he was the greatest master in the world. The Devil introduced himself and bade his new recruit follow. He did all the Devil asked of him until one day as they rode along a much used path they came in sight of a cross. Immediately the Devil left the path and rode through bushes and brambles making a wide detour to rejoin the path a mile farther on. Christopher asked the need for this.

'God became a man named Christ,' the Devil said, 'I influenced men to crucify Him, so now I am afraid when I see a Cross for it reminds me of Him.'

'Then it's good-bye to you,' said Christopher, 'for if you are afraid of Christ He must be greater than you, and I have sworn to serve only the greatest and best master,' and off he rode.

In his wanderings he met a hermit who told him much about Christ and Christopher said that he wanted to serve Him.

The hermit mentioned a river where many trying to ford it had fallen into deep pockets and been drowned.

'Because you are tall and strong,' the hermit said, 'live beside the river and help all who try to cross. In serving them you will be serving Christ, and He may come to see you.' Christopher went straight there, threw away his sword and took a staff to probe the depths of the river. He soon found the safest way through the water and was much in demand. Hundreds were grateful to him; the news spread, and soon it became the most popular point for crossing the river.

One day a child cried, 'Christopher, come and carry Me over, please.' Christopher did so but only after the most hazardous crossing that he had ever made.

'It felt as though I had the weight of the whole world on my shoulders, but why that should be I cannot tell,' he said.

'I will tell you,' the child said. 'The Person you have just carried over, made the world, and carries the sin of all the world.' Christopher asked to follow Christ, but He said, 'In serving others here you are serving Me.' Then Christopher knew he had to stay, but found pleasure in the knowledge that he had found the greatest and best of all masters.

Those of you who are leaving school to go to work will find that you will have to choose whether to serve the Devil or Christ. When you absent yourself without being sick, when you visit the toilet in work time for a smoke, when you take a small item from work, you are serving the evil one. But if you are honest, truthful, loyal and hard-working, then whatever the task, you are serving God, the greatest of all. A St. Christopher medallion won't keep you safe, but if you serve Christ you will be kept safe and you will prosper. King David served God and he reigned forty years, lived to a good old age, and was full of riches and honour. 'Who is willing to consecrate his service this day to the Lord?' Be like Christopher and serve the Lord in your daily task.

Prayer: Mighty God, help us to remember that whatever our work we must perform it as servants of Christ, so make us conscious of your presence and the power of the Holy Spirit strengthening us in our task, and give us joy in service. *Amen.*

35. *Olympic Games*

A PARABLE OF PEACE

Scripture Reading: Luke 2:8–19.
Key Verse: 14. Glory to God in the highest and on earth peace, goodwill toward men.
Hymn: Thy kingdom come, O God.

The Olympic Games; what thought does this conjure up in your mind? Do you see the huge stadium packed with onlookers and there on the track in the centre the fortunate competitors who have been chosen to represent their countries straining their hardest to be the best athlete in the world at their particular event? Do you hear the crowd shouting their countrymen on in different languages with the noise increasing and almost deafening you as the runners approach the tape? Or do you see the first three on the victory rostrum receiving their medals to the sound of their national anthems as their flags are hoisted, and wish that you were the victor? It could happen to you, for all the winners were schoolchildren once. The Olympic Games was a wonderful idea. Do you know how it started?

It all began in the valley of Olympia in southern Greece about three thousand years ago, nearly a thousand years before Jesus was born. Then every nation had its own god and Greece had many. The chief was called Zeus, the father of the gods, and a man called Heracles was the first to think of having a race in his honour. About 450 B.C. a statue of Zeus by the sculptor Pheidias was placed in a temple, and it became one of the Seven Wonders of the World. Sacrifices were made to this gold and ivory image of Zeus before the athletes walked to the near-by stadium to compete. At first there was only one race of about 200 yards but later the pentathlon was added and later still chariot racing and boxing. The victors were given a garland of leaves from an olive tree that Heracles planted.

After a few years other countries asked to take part and this the Greeks welcomed, but it posed one question. What about countries that were at war? All the competing countries agreed that when the Games were about to start a runner carrying a flaming torch would be the signal for all battles to cease. The participating countries were faithful to their promises and so it came about that there was peace during the Games. Unfortunately this doesn't happen now. The last two world wars have prevented the Games from being held.

There are records of the winners of these Games right back to 776 B.C., so it is possible that Isaiah saw this naked runner coming over the hills heralding peace, and this may have influenced him to say (52:7), 'How beautiful upon the mountains are the feet of him who brings good tidings that publish (proclaim) peace.' But Isaiah was speaking in prophecy of the Messiah, the One that God was promising to send into the world to bring peace, though not among nations so much as in the hearts of men.

Our reading today reminded us that God kept His promise at a time when His country was being ruled by a Roman governor. Jesus was born, and some shepherds heard an angel tell of His birth in the near-by village of Bethlehem. Suddenly other angels appeared and said, 'Glory to God in the highest and on earth peace, goodwill toward men.' The shepherds went and found the baby Jesus just as the angel had said, and they worshipped Him and then told everyone they met about the good news that God had sent His Son to bring peace to men.

This message of peace is still going around the world today, that God's Son came to forgive our sins to make peace between us and God the Father. When we believe this our guilty consciences go and peace comes to our hearts.

You will notice that the text says first, 'Glory to God in the highest,' and then 'peace upon earth' follows it. There is no peace in our hearts until we first glorify God by believing that Jesus died for our sins so that we might be forgiven. When you next hear about the runner with the torch who comes to start the Olympic Games, remember he was the signal for all fighting to cease. So was Jesus a herald of peace.

Prayer: O Lord Jesus Christ, we thank you for making peace between us and God the Father. Kindle in our hearts a real love for peace that we may glorify your Name. *Amen.*

36. True Worship

A PARABLE OF PRAISE

Scripture Reading: Matthew 21:14–17.
Key Verse: 16. Out of the mouths of babes and sucklings thou hast perfected praise.
Hymn: Praise, my soul, the King of heaven.

Did you join in that hymn? Were you just singing and not thinking about the meaning of the words, or were you really praising God because you have so much to thank him for? Praising God is more than joining in a hymn or a prayer, it is meaning with all your heart and soul what you sing or say to God. Perhaps you think that the praise of a child is so poor that God doesn't care much about it.

Robert Browning wrote a poem called, 'The boy and the angel' about just that. Theocrite was a craft apprentice who loved God and loved his work and so was happy all the day long. Frequently he would cry out, 'Praise God!', for he felt he had to express his gratitude to God for all his goodness towards him whether it was morning, evening, noon or night. A monk who used to watch him at his work said that God appreciated his praise just as much as the Pope's. Theocrite wished desperately that he was the Pope so that he could praise God better, in spite of the monk's words.

In a dream one day an angel came to him and told him that his desire would be granted and he would one day be the Pope. So he left his craft and became a student and then a priest and eventually Pope. Meanwhile the archangel Gabriel was anxious that God shouldn't miss young Theocrite's praise, so he took his place and praised God for him. As an angel it didn't matter to him what he did so long as he was serving God. But God said that He missed the little human praise that used to come from the heart of the boy. When the angel told Theocrite this he gave up his position as Pope and went back to his craft and to praising God as he used to do when a boy. You don't need to be the Archbishop of Canterbury to praise God. God truly loves the praise of a child.

The poet must have had in mind one of the verses that we read this morning: 'Out of the mouths of babes and sucklings hast thou perfected praise,' which means, 'The most beautiful form of praise is the kind that springs from the heart of a grateful child.'

When children saw Jesus in the temple healing the blind and the lame they shouted out their praise to Him because they were so happy for the people who had been healed. But the chief priests and the scribes whose duty it was to lead the worship in the temple when they heard this they protested that the children should not be encouraged to do this. It was then that Jesus reminded the priests that the psalmist had said that perfect praise came from the smallest of children.

It isn't who we are or what age we are or how important we are that counts with God. He looks into our hearts and knows if we truly love Him and whether we sincerely mean what we sing or say to Him. Remember that God misses your praise when you forget or are too busy to think about praising Him. But when you burst into praise because your heart is so full of happiness and gratitude to God, then this makes God very happy. The chief end of man is to glorify God. Will you join in our prayer of praise to God by listening to the words and if you mean them by saying 'Amen' at the end?

Prayer: Almighty God, the giver of all good things, we want to really thank you for all your love and goodness to us. We thank you for making us and keeping us and for the very many blessings we enjoy, but most of all we want to thank you for sending Jesus to save us from our sins and the hope of heaven that He has brought us. Help us to appreciate your many kindnesses so that our hearts may be truly thankful and we may praise you not only by what we say but by the way that we live and serve you. This we ask through Jesus Christ our Lord. *Amen.*

37. *Don't Waste Time*

A PARABLE OF THE END OF TERM

Scripture Reading: Ecclesiastes 3:1–13.
Key Verse: Ephesians 5:16. Redeeming the time . . .
Hymn: Lord, dismiss us with thy blessing . . .

Mary Hopkin has made very popular a song about there being a time for every purpose under the sun. The words were taken from the Bible reading that we had this morning. What the song and the Preacher is saying is, 'Don't waste time.' You may be looking forward to the end of term as 'a time to play,' but what about the term just past which was 'a time to work?' Have you spent this term well or have you just spent it, wasted it?

Your report book will tell you and your parents, whether you have wasted any time or not. There will be the record of your absences, genuine or not. I remember Tommy who was away the first four days of one week for no good reason but came on the Friday because he had heard that his form was going on a trip up the river and found that the other children had brought slips from their parents saying that they had their parents' permission. As he had no such slip Tommy had to remain in school and work on his own. Have you a full attendance?

Then there is the report on punctuality. Johnny was always arriving late for school because he dawdled on the way. One day his class was going to Twickenham to see the Oxford and Cambridge rugby match. Though he had determined to be on time he arrived just as the coach drove out of the school gates. Only one minute late, but too late. Are you never late?

Perhaps your parents will be more interested in the many subject reports. What will yours be like? 'Excellent' or 'Very good' or mostly 'Fair', which means, 'Not good enough'?

You will be just as pleased or as miserable as your parents with your report. Could it have been better if you hadn't wasted so much time?

The report that interests me most is the one on conduct, because that affects the whole of your report. You may be good at a certain subject but you will only get a poor mark in it if you waste time by being inattentive. A well-behaved child will get the most possible out of each subject and so get the best possible subject and conduct reports. Such a child won't play truant or be late and so will have a good all-round report that will please him and his parents, and me.

Ask yourself, 'If I could have this term over again would I do exactly the same?' Be honest in your reply. Has there not been some wasted time which cannot be recaptured no matter how much you wish it? Whenever I see a fountain where the water pours endlessly from the hands of a stone child and runs away into the pool, I think of the water as time, for so many folk let time flow through their hands and don't make use of it.

The Ephesians were like this and Paul had to remind them to 'Redeem the time,' or in other words, 'Make the most of each opportunity as it comes.' Think of the many opportunities that you have each day in school to improve your mind, body and spirit, or your knowledge, physique and conduct.

Are you ready for each opportunity as it comes along? Galileo looked at the eye of an ox, saw a lens, and today we have telescopes and microscopes because he saw an opportunity and used it. Columbus noticed that some branches which washed up on the shore were unusual. He investigated and discovered that they came from no known tree in the world. From this he deduced that there were countries as yet undiscovered and so set sail and discovered the New World. This helped to prove that the world was round at a time when it was thought flat. Watt noticed steam lift the lid of an iron kettle. From this he went on to put the power in steam into use and the steam-engine resulted. These three men, like many others, redeemed the time, made full use of it, didn't waste it, grasped the opportunity. 'I shall pass through this world but once. Any good thing that I can do, let me do it now. Let me not defer it nor neglect it, for I shall not pass this way again.'

Prayer: O God we thank you for the blessings of this term; forgive us for the time we have wasted and strengthen us in the holidays so we may return to work with new vigour and determination to redeem the time next term. *Amen.*

38. A Costly Gift

A PARABLE OF GRATITUDE

Scripture Reading: Luke 21:1–4.
Key Verse: 4 . . . cast in all the living she had.
Hymn: Now thank we all, our God . . .

Jesus had been telling His disciples about the Scribes who liked to be recognized in the streets, and sit in the most important seats in the church and at weddings and to make a show of long prayers in a meeting, yet would take the last penny from a widow even if it meant that she couldn't pay her rent. Then He pointed out a poor widow who put two mites equal to a farthing or a quarter of one penny into the offering box, and said that she had put in more than all the rest because she had put in every coin she had, all the money she had to buy food and all that she needed. This is real gratitude. Do you give like that?

We have no farthings now, or even halfpennies, but I can remember buying a long strip of liquorice for a farthing when I was a boy. A Scots lad of eleven years of age had been working hard at school so that he could go to a famous public school, and heard that he had passed the entrance examination so was very grateful to God and wondered how he could show it. The next Sunday in church, the minister asked the congregation to give generously that morning as they had to make a big down payment before the builders would start work on the new church hall. The following Sunday the treasurer thanked the people for the sum of £200 0s. 0¼d., which they had donated the previous Sunday morning. He said that the £200 had been paid to the contractors, but he didn't know what use the farthing was, but doubtless God knew. The farthing became quite a joke.

One of the deacons of the church explained it to the

pastor, 'Last Sunday, when you made your appeal for generous giving, my little son whispered to me that he had 4¼d and asked if he might put in the silver threepenny-piece. A moment later he said he wanted to put in the penny as well. On the way home he told me that he felt the farthing burning a hole in his pocket so he put that in the collection as well. He was so grateful to God that he put in all that he had. Now you know how the farthings got into the offering.'

This story of gratitude so pleased the minister that he told it to the worshippers at the next service, and he reminded them of the widow's mites in Jesus' story.

At the close of the meeting a stranger came to the pastor and asked if the story was true. The minister took him to Donald and got the boy to tell his own story. Of course it agreed exactly with what the minister had said. 'I'm sorry for doubting your word,' the stranger said, 'but it sounded too good to be true. Now that I know the truth of it I feel that God led me here this morning just to hear this story, for God has permitted me to prosper in my work and I have never once returned thanks to God in a practical way. This lad has taught me a lesson I needed to learn.' Then he took out his pen and wrote out a cheque for an amount that was sufficient to meet the total cost of the new hall. As he handed it to the minister he said, 'This may seem a large sum to you but it hasn't cost me as much as it cost Donald, for he gave all that he had.'

Do you consider that you are a grateful person? How often do you thank your mother for her love and care of you? Or do you think that it is her duty and she doesn't need any thanks? How often do you thank God for all his mercies towards you? Have you thanked Jesus for giving all that He had, His very life, to save you from the penalty for your sin? Let us show our gratitude to God now.

Prayer: O God, we thank you for our health and strength; for the air we breathe, for the good food that sustains us, for happy homes and loving parents, and for everything that makes life good. Most of all we thank you for Jesus who gave His life for us. Help us to show our gratitude by offering up all we have, our very lives, to be lived in your service in the power of the Holy Spirit, and for the sake of Jesus Christ our Lord. *Amen.*

39. All the Saints

A PARABLE OF LEADERSHIP

Scripture Reading: Joshua 1:1–9.
Key Verse: 5. As I was with Moses so I will be with you.
Hymn: For all the saints.

When Egypt was part of the British Empire a rebellion broke out at Tel-el-Kebir and an army under General Wolseley was sent to quell it. But he didn't know the way. A young lieutenant named Rawson, with only the stars to guide him, led the whole army safely and directly. The enemy and the rebellion were put down. In the fighting Rawson was seriously wounded and the General was quick to go to him. The lieutenant asked him, 'Didn't I lead you straight sir?' Wolseley was glad to answer, 'Yes, you did.' His good leadership ensured success.

Isn't this true in ordinary life? As children we have our heroes, those we admire and seek to imitate. But it is important that we choose the right ones to follow, because we shall finish where they lead us. The children who followed Bill Sykes in the story of 'Oliver Twist' ended up in real trouble because they copied his ways of picking other people's pockets. Bill himself finished on a rope's end.

Years ago many lads took Stanley Matthews as their soccer idol and copied his devotion to physical fitness, ball control and good sportsmanship and now are professional footballers. Today you copy men like Bobby Moore or George Best.

If we want to climb mountains who better to follow than Lord Hunt, Hilary or Tensing? They conquered the highest mountain in the world, Everest. They can teach us about *endurance.*

To learn *courage* we must look to someone like Ignatius of

Antioch who in the second century was torn to pieces by lions because he refused to deny his faith in Jesus Christ.

William Tyndale can teach us about *determination*, for he translated the New Testament so that Englishmen could read and understand it for themselves, and after most of the copies were appropriated and burnt and he was put in prison, he continued to translate the Old Testament right up to the moment when he was taken out and burnt at the stake for it.

Do we lack *compassion*? Let us look at Sir Philip Sidney who when sorely wounded gave the drink of water he so badly needed to a dying soldier, saying, 'Your need is greater than mine.'

Is it *love of freedom* that we need? We can look to William Wilberforce, who, as a member of Parliament, kept fighting the recognition of slavery until Britain renounced it once for all, even though that injustice was a source of wealth to so many.

For *dedication* we need to follow Kagawa, who persisted in working for better conditions for the poor of Japan until his objects were achieved.

Lord Shaftesbury had a *conscience* we all should want. It led him to fight for the poor children who climbed inside chimneys to sweep them, and who worked long hours in coal-mines, until he got a law passed forbidding child-labour.

So we could go on. We could make a long list of leaders to follow, but there is an easier way. They all had one thing in common which gave them their qualities. They all believed in Jesus Christ and followed Him. So all we need to do is to follow their example in following Him.

After Moses' death God spoke to the new leader of the Children of Israel, and told him that as He was with Moses so He would be with him. God advised him to obey His laws as they were written in the scriptures and He would lead them into the Promised Land. Success was assured if Joshua followed God.

When Jesus came hundreds of years later, He said, 'I am

in the Father and the Father in Me.' This is why He could say, 'Follow Me.' To follow Jesus is to follow God. In Him are all the virtues we have seen in many different people. Where you finish depends on whom you follow; Sykes to the scaffold, Matthews to Wembley, or Hilary to the top of Everest. To get to heaven we must follow Christ. And He is with us in the journey.

Prayer: Almighty and everlasting God, we thank you for those who have gone before and have set us such good examples to follow. Help us to follow your guidance as they did, so that we, in turn, may lead others to put their trust in you also, and become true disciples of your Son, our Saviour Jesus Christ. *Amen.*

40. Lionheart or Francis?

A PARABLE OF COURAGE

Scripture Reading: 2 Corinthians 11:23–27.
Key Verse: 12:9. My grace is sufficient for you.
Hymn: He who would valiant be.

Today there is much talk about the Holy Land and which nation has the right to inhabit it, Jew or Arab. Ever since Jesus lived there men have argued and fought over it. We have all heard of King Richard the Lionheart who spent much of his time fighting to recover the Holy Land from the Turks. Palestine was sacred to Christians as Christ's native land, so when Mohammedans entered and killed Christian pilgrims the whole Christian Church in Europe, under the Pope, was ready to fight to win it back. This went on for about 200 years in the Middle Ages, and each attempt to do this was called a crusade. Richard started out with two other kings but they let him down and he had to fight with only his own men. At a cost of many lives he got the enemy leader Saladin to promise not to interfere with any Christians who were visiting the Holy Land as pilgrims. Richard's title of Lionheart shows that he had a great deal of courage. He believed that God would help him to defeat the enemy with his sword so that Christian pilgrims could worship their God on soil that was sacred to them.

Another man of this crusade was Francis of Assisi. Born of rich parents, he took a commission in the army and gave little thought to others until he was seriously wounded in battle and feared death and what would follow as a result of his selfish life. On being restored to health he sold all his goods and gave the proceeds to the church and the poor. He worked at repairing old churches and preached the gospel to anyone who would listen. Soon he gained a band of followers and they all lived in poverty caring for the sick and needy.

All this showed another kind of courage. News of the great slaughter of Christians and Mohammedans reached Francis and he was deeply concerned for them all. He said, 'We shan't conquer the Sultan by force, but only by love, and I am willing to risk my life to prove it.' Some asked to go with him and he took a small band but they took no weapons and wore their usual grey habit which made it clear that they were not soldiers. They travelled with the Crusaders until they reached the borders of Palestine and then he and one other went into the enemy lines alone. On the way they sang the 23rd Psalm '. . . though I walk through the valley of the shadow of death I will fear no evil, for thou art with me.' When they reached a Saracen camp they were roughly handled and bound and taken to the officer in charge. To him Francis said, 'I am a Christian sent by God. Take me to the one who gives you your orders.' This was done several times until at last Francis stood before the Sultan himself. Then he told the Saracen leader of the love of Jesus Christ, God's Son, for all men. The Sultan was so surprised by the courage and sincerity of Francis that he asked him to stay. Francis said he would if the Mohammedans promised to worship Christ. This the Sultan was not prepared to do, but because he admired Francis' courage he gave him safe escort to near the Christian camp. The Sultan's last words to him were, 'Pray for me that God will show me what is the true faith.' We too must admire such courage as this.

We may not be asked to show the same sort of courage as Richard Lionheart, or that of Francis, or to go through the perils that Paul had to suffer for Christ's sake, but if we recognize that these men got their courage from God we shall know where to go to find the same.

We shall need courage to stand up for that which is good and true and right. We may need to stand up to those who laugh at our beliefs. For this we shall need courage. Let us remind ourselves that God will give us the courage he gave to Lionheart and Francis and Paul, and Joshua, and Gideon, and David, and all the others who trusted in him. He said, 'My grace is sufficient for you,' and that means you.

Prayer: Strengthen us, O God, in all the hazards of life and in trials and temptations, and give us the courage of Him who faced the Cross, that like Him we may be found faithful to the end. For the sake of Jesus Christ our Lord. *Amen.*

41. F. D. Roosevelt

A PARABLE OF FIGHTING

Scripture Reading: 1 Timothy 6:8–12.
Key Verse: 11. Follow after righteousness, godliness, faith, love, patience, meekness. Fight the good fight of faith.
Hymn: Fight the good fight.

In Grosvenor Square, London, there stands a statue of a man who helped us win the last war. He was the President of the United States of America, Franklin Delano Roosevelt, and all his life was one long fight. He was Assistant Secretary to the U.S. Navy in the First World War, and it was said of him that he fought as hard as any sailor on a warship.

One summer's day in 1921, he took his sons sailing, but they noticed a forest fire and returned to shore to help fight it. It was hot, exhausting work so they went for a swim afterwards. Returning home, Roosevelt found that a lot of mail had come, so he sat down in his wet costume to read his letters. When he had finished reading he felt very cold and his limbs were numb. He was paralysed and there was no known cure, but he decided to fight it. For three years there was no improvement. Then he heard of a young man who had been cured of paralysis by exercising in the water at Warm Springs, Georgia. So he went, and after a long and patient fight he felt a little better. Newspaper reporters wanted to write that he had been cured, but Roosevelt fought them on this and made them promise to tell the truth. Many sufferers with infantile paralysis, hearing the news, flocked to Warm Springs grasping at any ray of hope. But there wasn't room for them, so Roosevelt had some old cottages renovated and made suitable for cripples. Later he fought to keep the Springs for healing and had to buy them to achieve his end.

He was so concerned at the state of affairs in New York that he decided to forget about the hope of a cure for himself, and sought the Governorship of the town. This he achieved, and it led on to his election to the Presidency of the United States. This was in 1932 when there had been a world slump which had badly affected America. There was much unemployment and banks were unable to pay back the money that people had deposited with them. Roosevelt saw that the unemployment got relief and promised bank depositors full repayment eventually. Then he arranged a Government partnership with industry, housing, transport and agriculture. This great fight against national poverty was so successful that he was re-elected with an overwhelming majority in 1936.

This took him to 1940, by which time we in Britain were fighting to save our country from Nazi domination. Once more Roosevelt was made President, and immediately he took steps to help us all that he could. He sent destroyers and ammunition and devised a Lease-Lend scheme by which we, and our allies, could have all we needed without paying for it until after the war. In 1941 the Americans came to fight side by side with us. They were prominent in the invasion of Normandy in 1944 which began just before the end of Roosevelt's third term of office and no one was surprised when this successful fighter was elected as President for a fourth term.

His last great fight was against war altogether. At the Yalta conference with Winston Churchill and Stalin, he sought to arrange an international conference in order to form a world organization to settle differences between nations without going to war. Peace came soon after his death. And so this longest-serving of all United States Presidents, this man whose life was one long fight against sickness, wrongdoing, unbelief, hatred, impatience, poverty and arrogance, ended with a fight for peace and freedom.

He must have known Paul's advice to Timothy, 'Follow after righteousness, godliness, faith, love, patience, meekness and fight the good fight of faith,' for he had lived up to it all.

Let us determine that we too shall fight as our faith in God tells us to do.

Prayer: O God, give us such a love for you that we may love goodness and truth and justice which come from you alone. Strengthen us to fight, not one another, but all that is evil and base. Make us ever ready to help all who suffer poverty, oppression and injustice, that our love of others may point them to Him who is the King of Love and the Prince of Peace. *Amen.*

42. *A Fourth Person*

A PARABLE OF THE NEW YEAR

Scripture Reading: Daniel 3:8–25.
Key Verse: Matthew 28:20. I am with you always, even to the end.
Hymn: O God, our help in ages past . . .

Ernest Shackleton, a young man of twenty-nine years was very disappointed. He had been one member of an expedition to the South Pole but had broken down on a sledging journey and had been forced to return home. But he was not daunted. Five years later he was invited to lead another expedition and was quick to accept it. This time he did much better. He got to within ninety-seven miles of the pole, and planted a Union Jack on Mount Gauss, the nearest any man had ever been to this pole. For this he was knighted in 1909.

Naturally, he was asked to command the Imperial Trans-Antartic Expedition which began in 1914. Though he was not taking any part in the Great War, his assignment was more hazardous than the average soldier was given. The object was to cross the continent from one side to the other, from the Weddell Sea to the Ross Sea. But the project completely failed when his ship, the *Endurance*, stuck in the ice and when it began to break up had to be abandoned. The twenty-eight men made a perilous journey over drifting ice, and when it started to break up they had to row sixty miles in small boats to Elephant Island. Most of the men stayed on this barren island whilst Shackleton with five others went on in a twenty-two-foot boat to the nearest whaling station. This was 750 miles away and it took sixteen days, through cold, stormy weather.

Imagine their disappointment when, on reaching South Georgia they found that their boat would not last long enough to reach the farther side of the island where the whaling-station was. Shackleton took the two fittest men and they 'had to climb up to the rugged peaks of the South Georgian Mountains over the glaciers down to the far side and the whaling station. This took a day and a half, and in their distressed condition was the worst part of all their journeying. A boat was sent which picked up the men on the far side of the island and those who had been left on Elephant Island.

Shackleton wrote a book about this expedition and of this last part he said that during the long racking march from one side of South Georgia to the other, when all were too tired to speak, and their thoughts were about their closeness to death, in the absolute silence, they felt that there was someone with them.

Shackelton died at this island on the next expedition from a heart attack after influenza.

The sensing of a fourth person with them has been made by others who have travelled over lonely areas, and many have felt such a Presence when in deep meditation on their own or in times of great danger.

Our Bible story this morning told of Shadrach, Meshack and Abed-nego, who endured the flames of a fierce furnace sooner than worship an idol. They said, 'Our God is able to deliver us, but if not, we will not bow down to the idol.' Such faith as this got its reward. They came out of the furnace unharmed. The king said that he saw one other, a fourth person with them like unto the Son of God. They knew that their God would not let them down if they were faithful to Him.

Jesus before His ascension said to His disciples, 'Go and preach the gospel, and I will be with you always.' We can be sure, if we believe in God, that He will be with us at all times, and that means throughout this New Year. There is no problem that you will have that He cannot solve, no danger that He cannot bring you through. You are never alone if you really believe that the main reason for Jesus permitting His crucifixion, resurrection and ascension was so that His Spirit might be with all His children all the days.

Perhaps we should ask God to open our eyes so that we might recognize His Presence.

Prayer: At the commencement of this New Year we ask your presence with us O God, to guide us with your wisdom and to protect us with your love, in each and every day. Help us to recognize your presence at least at each assembly. *Amen.*

43. Age of Miracles

A PARABLE OF SICKNESS

Scripture Reading: Matthew 8:1–17.
Key Verse: 17. He took our infirmities and bore our sicknesses.
Hymn: O for a thousand tongues to sing . . .

John said that Jesus came to destroy the works of the Devil (1 John 3:8), and Jesus said that sickness was the work of the Devil. This means that one of Jesus' reasons for coming to earth was so that we might not stay sick, and we know that He healed the sick whenever He was asked to do so. Every time He told His disciples to preach the gospel He told them to heal the sick too. This they did and raised the dead as well. Jesus prophesied that His followers would do even greater things than He did, and this has come to pass from time to time. In this present day hundreds of thousands of people have received Divine healing. At other times when faith in God has waned, people have had to seek other means of healing. So there has grown up a body of doctors and nurses which has sought to aid the sick by earthly means. But whether you get your healing from a doctor's hands or direct from God in a simple answer to prayer, God is in it. Any doctor will tell you that he cannot cure any sickness; all he can do is to assist in the natural healing process that God built into us when he made us. Let me tell you of one example of each kind of healing.

A girl was lying seriously ill in a cottage in Devonshire, and the doctor was called in. He told the mother, 'Only a miracle can save her. I can do nothing.' The little sister, hearing this, picked up her money-box and ran to the general stores. The shopkeeper was in conversation with a distinguished-looking gentleman, but the little girl couldn't wait. She pulled the proprietor's apron and said, 'Please, I want to buy a miracle.' The shopkeeper said, 'I'm sorry, but I don't sell miracles,' and the child began to cry. The gentleman asked her why she wanted a miracle and she told him. 'Take me to your sister,' he said and she led him home. He explained to the parents that he was a surgeon at a famous London hospital, away on holiday, and said that he would like to help. The local doctor borrowed some instruments from the hospital and the surgeon performed an operation that saved the sister's life.

T. L. Osborn is a missionary who has visited more than forty countries, and wherever he has preached the gospel many people have received healing from all kinds of sicknesses when he has prayed for them. At one campaign meeting in Trinidad many hundreds of people were being healed and a cripple lad was given faith to believe that God would do the same for him. His name was Harold Khan. One leg had been broken and as a result it was 5¼ inches shorter than the other. He had irons on the leg to support it and had to walk with the aid of a crutch. He was so sure that the same Jesus who had cured the lame when He was on earth, was alive then and would heal him, that he took off his leg-irons and put down his crutch. God honoured his faith. As T. L. Osborn prayed, Harold's leg grew 5¼ inches, and both legs were strengthened so that he was able to run around on the platform before the eyes of thousands, and after thanking God, he went off to play his favourite game of football once more.

If we believe as Harold did then we shall see miracles of Divine healing. The prophet Isaiah foretold that when Christ came He would take our infirmities and bear our sicknesses for us, and would be flogged by the Roman soldiers, and because of those stripes we should be healed. And it is coming true today, wherever people believe it. The Age of Miracles is not past.

God intends people to be healed by simple faith in His Son Jesus Christ. But because His mercy is so great He brings relief through doctors and medicine to those who don't believe in Him.

Prayer: O Lord Jesus Christ, we know that You came to bring to each one of us a full, abundantly healthy life. At those times when sickness comes upon us, give us faith to believe that You will heal us. We pray for those that we know are ill and ask You, in simple faith, to make them well, so that Your Name may be glorified. *Amen.*

44. Archbishop or King?

A PARABLE OF FORGIVENESS

Scripture Reading: Matthew 18:21–35.
Key Verse: Matthew 6:14. If you forgive men their trespasses your heavenly Father will also forgive your trespasses.
Hymn: The Son of God goes forth to war.

William Wallace was one of Scotland's national heroes. He lived in the thirteenth century at a time when Scotland was under the yoke of England. As a young man he was insulted by an Englishman and in the fight that ensued he killed him. This made him an outlaw and he had to keep moving from place to place. Many of those Scots who helped him to hide from the English eventually were outlawed themselves and so he gathered a small band of men who started guerilla activities against the hated Englishmen. Wallace was so successful that other groups were formed under his leadership, until a large portion of Scotland was in rebellion. Scottish nobles joined his band but they deserted when an English army came over the border to disperse them. Despite this Wallace faced the soldiers and won the battle of Stirling Bridge, and then went on to drive the English out of Scotland. Even then he didn't stop but devastated most of Northern England.

The Scots gloried in this and Wallace was elected guardian of Scotland. King Edward determined that this leader of rebels must be caught and punished and himself led a very large army which scattered Wallace's forces but he didn't catch Wallace. This great defeat caused the nobles to withdraw their support and Wallace was forced to return to the small forays for the next few years. Eventually he was caught and brought to London and sentenced to death by hanging as a traitor.

A poem by Blind Harry records that Wallace asked if he might have a priest so that he might confess his sins and ask God's forgiveness in order that he might go to heaven. King Edward not only refused this request but threatened to hang any priest who ministered to Wallace in this way. He would not forgive Wallace and didn't intend to let God forgive him if that were at all possible.

All the lesser priests that were there hung back for fear of their lives, but the Archbishop of Canterbury stepped forward and told the King that this was one thing he could deny no man. According to Blind Harry, the Archbishop told the King that he would declare him a heretic if he interfered. He then proceeded to shrive Wallace and knelt on the stones of Smithfield with him as he prepared to meet his God. Doubtless the Archbishop remembered the words of Jesus, who when asked about obeying a king or ruler said, 'Render unto Caesar the things that are Caesar's and unto God the things that are God's.' Jesus was saying that in a conflict between the commands of a king or those of God, God should be put first. This the Archbishop did. He remembered the words of Jesus that if we do not forgive those who do wrong to us then God will not forgive our sins against him. It would seem from this story of Blind Harry that King Edward will not be excused by God for not forgiving Wallace.

How many times should we forgive people who offend us? After all, Wallace did constantly murder Englishmen and would have gone on doing it if he hadn't been caught. But when Peter asked if he should forgive seven times, Jesus replied, 'Seventy times seven,' and by this He meant that there is no limit to forgiveness.

If we want God to go on forgiving us for all our sins then we must go on being forgiving to other people.

Prayer: The Lord's Prayer (remembering especially the phrase, 'Forgive us our trespasses as we forgive those who trespass against us').

45. *The Mean Cooper*

A PARABLE OF PENITENCE

Scripture Reading: Mark 1:1–15.
Key Verse: 15. Repent and believe the gospel.
Hymn: Father of heaven, whose love profound . . .

Have you ever been to Alum Bay in the Isle of Wight? If you have, then you will almost certainly have bought a little test-tube and filled it with the many different coloured sands of which the cliffs are formed. Up in the Scottish Highlands there is a very clear pool which has many different coloured sands on its bed, and on sunny days these many colours are clearly visible. The local people tell a legend about folk who wanted to change the colour of their clothes, taking them to the lake and leaving them with a little gift for the fairies and a prayer for the colour that they desired. In the morning when they returned they found their clothes beautifully dyed.

But the story isn't finished. One day a shepherd having shorn his sheep brought the fleece from a black sheep and left it by the pool with a prayer for it to be turned white. When he returned the next morning he found the fleece still black. This is the reason why if you tried it now you wouldn't succeed, the locals say, for the fairies couldn't turn black white and so left the pool in despair. Our best chemists can make many coloured dyes from black coal-tar, but they cannot make black clothes white.

King David committed a terrible sin and he felt dirty in God's sight, and prayed, 'Wash me, and I shall be whiter than snow.' But there is more to it than that. We need to do more than just call on God to do a cleaning job for us. He is very willing to do this, for He likes us to be pure and clean, but first He wants to know that we are really sorry for our sins, the things that blackened our characters. I expect at some time you have done something that your mother had said you were not to do and she has said that you would be punished, and you have been very quick to say, 'I'm sorry, Mum,' so that she would forgive you. Perhaps too you have done the wrong thing once more and she has said that she wouldn't forgive you this time unless you really meant it when you said that you were sorry. God is like this too.

Another legend tells of a mean barrel-maker. One day, when in his workshop with the doors open because of the heat of the day, a poor beggar stopped to ask him for a drink of water, but the cooper replied, 'I never give anything to people who are too lazy to work for a living. There is a fountain in the town, get your drink there.'

The little, stooping beggar drew himself up to his full height and, in a voice that sounded like thunder, roared, 'You miserly wretch, I shall punish you for this. You will roll your biggest barrel to the fountain, fill it to the brim and then bring it back to me. You will not be able to do any more work until you have done this task for me.'

The cooper laughed and went to pick up a tool to continue his work but found he could not. He tried to turn away but couldn't. When he took a step in the direction of the fountain he found this to be quite natural. And so, because he could do nothing but walk to the fountain he did so, rolling the great barrel as he went. When he got there he tried to fill the barrel but found no water would enter it. He tried pouring water and dipping the barrel under the water but no water went in. After half an hour of this he felt very desperate. Would he be forced to do this for the rest of his life? He knew that he was being punished for his lack of charity and knew that he deserved it. He so really and truly was sorry for his sin that he began to cry and one of his tears fell into the barrel and then another until it seemed that he would fill the barrel with his tears. Then he tried dipping the barrel under the water once more and found that it filled quite naturally. This is what Jesus meant when He said, as John the Baptist had said before Him, 'Repent.'

Repentance, or penitence as it is sometimes called, means

more than just saying we are sorry for our wrong-doing, it means turning round and facing the other way, doing the very opposite of our wrong-doing, showing that we are sincere in saying we are sorry by seeing that we never do that wrong thing ever again; real sorrow for our sin. When we repent we can be sure that Jesus will forgive us and wash us clean no matter how black our sins are.

Prayer: Create in me a clean heart O God and renew a right spirit within me and forgive me all my sins. *Amen.*

46. A Smile and a Song

A PARABLE OF JOY

Scripture Reading: Acts 16:22–34.
Key Verse: 34 he rejoiced, believing in God.
Hymn: Rejoice the Lord is King.

Everybody in the school knew Henry Fawcett. He was very popular with the boys and not so popular with the teachers because he was always making the boys laugh in class. One day the class roared out loud, and when the master said, 'And what is it this time Fawcett?' Henry replied, 'I can't think what made them laugh sir, I only said that I was going to be a Member of Parliament.' Even the master smiled. But this was typical of Henry; he was so full of joy that nothing could upset his good humour.

One day, out shooting with his father, he saw some partridges start up and fly over the next field. In trying to prevent this happening a second time Henry was shot in the face and was blinded for life. Despite the pain he put a smiling face on it. And he went on doing everything that he had done before, skating, fishing and studying to become that M.P. he had promised himself he would be. And he made it. He was loved by the working-class people as he did so much for them, and the cab-drivers refused to take his fare saying it was such fun to drive him home. Never once was he sorry for himself and always made others happy by his presence.

During the Great War the Tommies, as our soldiers were called, marched into battle singing, 'Pack up your troubles in your old kit bag, and smile, smile, smile.' This was the cheerful courage which kept their morale high and helped to make them victorious.

Robert Louis Stevenson was sick for most of his life but was never sad. In great pain, in a darkened room, and lying on his right side by doctor's orders, so unable to use his right hand for writing, he nevertheless wrote with his left hand, 'We should all be as happy as kings.'

What made these people so happy in spite of trouble? Perhaps it was the same as with John Newton the captain of a slave-trading vessel who became a Christian and found his life transformed from sadness to joy. In one of the hymns that he wrote he told the secret of his inward happiness; 'With Christ in the vessel I smile at the storm.' If we let Christ into our lives we shall find joy even in adversity.

Look at Paul and Silas. They were thrown into prison after being given a flogging, and put in the stocks, yet they sang hymns because even physical pain couldn't drive out the joy that was in their hearts for love of Christ. This must have impressed their jailor. When an earthquake came and opened up the prison, the jailor took his sword to commit suicide, for he was responsible to the authorities with his life for the safe-keeping of his prisoners. Paul shouted out, 'Don't harm yourself, we are all here.' This so amazed the officer that he asked the secret of their joy in sorrow, and refusal to take advantage of a chance to escape and asked what he should do to become as happy as they were. Paul told him that when you believe in the Lord Jesus Christ His joy becomes part of you. The scriptures record that the jailor believed in Paul's god and he rejoiced, which means that he expressed his joy.

How different this was from the story in Psalm 137 which tells how when the Children of Israel were in captivity in Babylon and asked by their guards to sing one of their hymns they said that they hadn't got the heart for it, and they hung their harps on the willow trees down by the banks of the river. That is the way people act when trouble comes. But not Henry Fawcett, or Robert Louis Stevenson or Paul or Silas, or for that matter any true Christian, for when you once know Jesus Christ you have a joy which is not of this world for it comes from Him especially to cheer us in our troubles. Believe on the Lord Jesus Christ and you will be saved and rejoice in that salvation all your days.

Prayer: O God, we thank you for all the good things of life that make us happy, and for showing us in the life of Jesus that His joy came from forgetting selfish desires. Help us to be so filled with His Holy Spirit that we may always rejoice in your loving care and provision. *Amen.*